AS GOOD AS YOUR WORD

AS GOOD AS YOUR WORD
A THIRD BOOK OF
CONTEMPORARY
PRAYERS

by
Caryl Micklem and Roger Tomes

edited by
Caryl Micklem

William B. Eerdmans Publishing Company
Grand Rapids, Michigan

Contents

Preface

Since the publication of *Contemporary Prayers for Public Worship* (1967) and *More Contemporary Prayers* (1970), a number of people have been kind enough to ask for a further collection, in form more like the first book than the second yet mindful of the more explicitly theological slant of the latter.

The present volume is an attempt to fulfil this request. It is intended as a resource-book for the preparation of acts of worship in church and school. We hope we have included prayers appropriate to most situations and occasions, though we have not thought it necessary to re-print such items as the Ascriptions of Glory and the Blessings from the first book.

We considered arranging the prayers in a series of complete 'menus', but decided in the end that grouping together prayers more or less of a kind would make the book more readily useful. The needs of schools, in particular, are so widely different as regards the brevity and informality of their worship-occasions that it seemed most practical simply to offer classified ingredients for the customer's own mix. At the same time we are very much aware that in the case of some of the more general prayers classification is rather arbitrary, and is to be taken as suggesting a starting-point rather than filling without remainder a slot of that particular name. There is a more detailed subject index at the end of the book.

Except in the one or two instances indicated in the text, the prayers have been composed by the compilers. If by some trick of memory we have unwittingly taken ideas or phrases from others, we apologize to them and hope that the fact that their work stuck so fast in our minds will gratify them enough to excuse us.

Finally, a word to those who will use this book for personal reading and devotion. In a number of instances it will be found that successive prayers in a section pick up a single phrase, often a biblical allusion. If this seems repetitious to the reader he is asked to understand that the intention here is to make selection easier for someone preparing worship, who, finding one prayer, says, 'That is not quite what I want: let me see if there is something else on similar lines.'

Prayers

I
Approach

1

Your mercies are new every morning: your faithfulness is great.
We praise you, O God, for your goodness to mankind; for the chance
    to live and the call to serve.
We praise you for Jesus Christ and all that he means to us.
Renew our sense of thankfulness in worship, and show us what you
    want of us.
Forgive our sins and banish our guilty fears.
Give us the zest to live in the present with joy, and enable us to commit
    the future confidently into your hands.

2

We begin our worship, Lord God, with a deep sense of gratitude for
our life, for the good things we enjoy, for the knowledge of Jesus
Christ. We have not earned these things: you have given them to us.
We do not deserve these things: our service is fitful and unsatis-
factory, and we are no better than many who are less well off than
ourselves. Yet we believe that the things we enjoy and the uneasy
feelings we do not enjoy are equally your gifts – to teach us to care, to
share what we have, not to be content with ourselves as we are. We
will hear what you have to say to us through this act of worship.
Encourage us, and give us the strong desire to do your bidding and
help fulfil your purpose.

3

Our God and Father, we worship you. In company with all who turn
towards you we adore you. Be close to our thoughts and prayers, so
that we may receive from you the blessing you are waiting to give us.
We confess the selfishness which mars our obedience to your will. We
have seen your glory in your Son, but we have not faithfully reflected
what we have seen. We have allowed anger and bitterness to get the
better of us, and have given in to temptation without a struggle.
Father, forgive us and help us. May we so follow Jesus in the way he
treads that we come out from the captivity of sin and find our freedom in his service. Keep us in the company of those who have faith.

4

Eternal God, Father of our Lord Jesus Christ, we praise you for everything you have done for mankind in him.
Have pity on our feeble efforts to make our lives match our beliefs. We
are ashamed. Make us determined to try again to live up to your
expectation of us. May the life and teaching of Jesus become the
measure by which we assess each day's events and opportunities.
Strengthen our intention to live responsibly in today's rich but
anguished world. And may the meeting of our minds here, and our
attempts to help each other to be obedient, make a place where
people find it easier to know you and believe in you.
Through Jesus Christ our Lord.

5

We worship you, the God who comes near.
We thank you that you have always loved the world you made.
Since you are here now, help us to look for you in the stillness and to
listen for you in the quiet.
Show yourself to us in the face of Jesus.
Speak to our hearts in the words of Jesus.
Fill our lives with the Spirit of Jesus.

6

Lord of light, send out your light and your truth. Let them lead us.
Let them bring us up towards your level, and towards the experience
of your presence. Grant that now and always we may offer you the
true worship of mind and heart, imagination and will.
Through Jesus Christ our Saviour.

7

'Worship is the quickening of the conscience by God's holiness.'
O God, you have called us to a high standard of conduct through the
commands of the law, through the warnings of your prophets,
through the teaching and example of Jesus, through the lives of
faithful Christians:
We confess how far short we have fallen and we ask your forgiveness.

'Worship is the nourishment of the mind with God's truth.'
We thank you, Lord, for all knowledge, and especially for the knowledge
of your love, which wins us and builds us up in Christian faith.

'Worship is the purifying of the imagination with God's beauty.'
You have created so much that is beautiful, Lord.
How beautiful you yourself must be!

'Worship is the opening of the heart to God's love.'
Father, we commend to you those whom you love and we love.
May our love to them help to reflect yours.

'Worship is the surrender of the will to God's purpose.'
Our Father . . .

(*Based on words of William Temple*)

8

Lord God, we worship you. When we look at the wonders of the earth
and the sea and the sky, we see some of the greatness of your power,
some of the marvels of your wisdom.

But it is when we look at the world of men, and consider how things go
  with our own lives, that we come to see our need of your pardon and
  your peace, and to understand some of the greatness of your love in
  sending us your Son, Jesus.
Remembering his life on earth, we realize again how far our lives fall
  short of the glory you intend for us.
Remembering his death on the cross, we ask to be forgiven for our sins
  and rescued from our sinfulness.
And remembering his resurrection and kingly reign, we pray for the
  Holy Spirit who is yours and his, so that what we do and say and
  think may bring credit upon the gospel.
Heavenly Father, keep us in your ways. When things are dark, let
  what you have done for us in Jesus Christ be a lamp for our feet and
  a light for our path. We ask it for his name's sake.

9

Heavenly Father, we thank you for your unchanging love; and we
  thank you for giving us one another, so that in the love we give and
  receive among the people who mean much to us we can learn to
  understand your love. We thank you that your love was most per-
  fectly seen in Jesus: and we pray for his spirit, in his name.

10

God, our heavenly Father, we worship you in thankfulness and praise.
  May the presence of each us here encourage the others, so that we
  may go forward in faith and hope and love.
Let this place set apart speak to us of that which knows no bounds –
  the heaven of your presence.
Let this time set apart speak to us of that which transcends time –
  the eternity of your love.
Let the things that we hear speak to us of things that cannot be told.
And let everything that we see help us to serve more truly you whom
  we cannot see.
Through Jesus Christ our Lord.

11

God our Father, we worship you with joy.
We believe that you welcome us, and have a place for us by your side,
    now and to all eternity.
It is Jesus who makes us sure of this, by the welcome he gave to all
    sorts of people, even sinners, and by saying that he was going to you
    to make ready for us.
So Jesus makes possible new birth into a living hope for all of us, if we
    follow his example and trust his love.
Father, have mercy on our stubborn hearts, so slow to believe, so quick
    to turn aside from the right path.
Have mercy on our hard hearts, so easily exhausted when it comes to
    compassion for others, so untiring when it comes to seeking our own
    advantage.
May the rescuer whom you have sent save us and set us free, so that we
    are no longer the slaves of sin but the willing servants of the Most
    High God – loving you, our Father, and our neighbour for your sake
    and in your way.
Through Jesus Christ our Lord.

12

Lord God, we who have come together to worship you are very differ-
    ent people. We are at various stages in our life, and our circum-
    stances vary. We are conscious of widely differing needs. It is
    difficult for the words of one of us to convey what we are all feeling.
And yet we are united by our common humanity. As we look at each
    other, we see what we were in days gone by, or what we shall be in
    days to come. We see the kind of person we might have been, or the
    kind of person we should like to be. And we could not do without
    each other. We need one another to talk to. We need to help and be
    helped.
And we are here because we have all sensed something of life's mystery
    and wonder. We feel thankful, and we reach out to the author of all
    good things. We feel responsible, and we want to give account to our
    maker.

We believe that we have seen something of the pattern for our life in Jesus Christ and those who have followed him. Help us to understand that pattern more fully and enable us to come nearer to it.

13

Lord our God, heavenly Father, we praise and adore you.
In the thoughts of our hearts each of us turns towards you; each of us asks forgiveness for evil things done and good things left undone.
And yet in our prayer and worship we are together: for we are all here in the name of Jesus; it is through Jesus that we have learnt to approach you; it is because of Jesus that we dare to do so. May the Holy Spirit who is yours and his give us joy and peace in this fellowship of faith: and may we through the worship of today be strengthened in understanding and resolve for the service of your kingdom.

14

Through the praise which we share with all your people, there comes to us, Lord, your own call to us, renewed day by day – the call to put our trust in you, and to believe that your love is stronger than all the things which dismay us, stronger even than death.
Lord, we believe; help us where faith falls short. We mean to trust; yet our fears remain.
Give us new courage now – from the Bible, and from one another, and from the silence and peace of this place.

(*A silence*)

Father, we have sinned against you and against our brother man.
Forgive us the wrongs of which our consciences accuse us; and forgive us the wrongs of which we are unaware, because habit condones them and society gives them its blessing.
Through Jesus Christ our Lord.

15

Heavenly Father, as our lips and voices frame your praise in words, take possession also of our hearts, our wills and our love. All in us that dishonours you, forgive and vanquish by your grace. Help us to bring not only ourselves but one another into your presence; and may your church, here and everywhere, be equipped by your Spirit for work in your service. May our meeting here today foreshadow the time, and hasten the time, when all men shall know and rejoice in you, the only true God, and Jesus Christ whom you have sent.

16

Heavenly Father, we are glad to be here again.
We are glad of one another's company, helping us to worship you.
We are glad of this place, where the things we see and hear remind us of you.
Help us to give you our full attention. May we not be content to worship you only at this time and place and with these people: but rather let us here make a new beginning in the way we mean to go on – seeking and serving you at every turn.
Father, when we go wrong – or when we forget you, which is to forget ourselves – deal gently but firmly with us, we pray. Bring us back to a right mind and a right path, through Jesus Christ our Lord.

17

Lord God, may your eternal light and your enduring truth lead us to your presence.
Speak with living voice to our hearts: speak, and let your servants hear.
We confess the sin which has so often made us heedless of your call.
We have thought too much of ourselves, and too little of others.
We have missed chances of doing good: often our words and actions have done harm.
Forgive us, Father, and set us free from the evil power of sin.
Bring us out from the narrow confines of self into the wide open spaces of companionship and compassion.

And may your Spirit among us enable us to make good use of the
liberty you give us.
Through Jesus Christ our Lord.

18

Lord Jesus Christ, you are light for all the world. Shine into our hearts,
so that our lives may be filled with light and truth. Help us to have
done with every thought or word or action which darkens the path
for someone else. We confess how often we have been makers of pain
and difficulty. Enable us instead to be makers of peace and joy –
your disciples and your messengers.
For your name's sake.

19

God our heavenly Father, we adore you. You are far greater than we
can imagine, yet your mercy is as great as your majesty. By your
love made known in the life and death of Jesus, you rescue men and
women from the power of darkness and bring them into light. All our
agonies and perplexities find understanding and pity at the Cross.
Help us to know and believe the love you have for all your children,
and to trust to that love for life, for death and for resurrection.

20

Father, while your praise is sung we are glad to feel part of it, and our
hearts are lifted up – we are in high spirits. But in the silence which
follows the telling of your greatness, we feel small. We are dwarfed
by your splendour and put to shame by your holiness. We have not
followed after goodness with our whole hearts. Often we have taken
no notice. Worse still, we have done actual harm – hurting one
another by our words and deeds. Help us to be big enough to ask
forgiveness from those we have wronged. We ask forgiveness from
you, our Father. Let your mercy towards us be as great as your
majesty: for the sake of Jesus Christ our Lord.

21

Lord, you are faithful to your promises and consistent in your purposes.
With you in the picture our human fickleness is shown up. For ourselves and for all our race we confess that we have not kept faith
with you or with one another.

> Lord, have mercy upon us . . .

As we open our hearts to you, do your saving and healing work within
us, and among us, and through us. May there be, in the Christian
fellowship, such an experience of your accepting love, that we in our
turn may learn how to love as you have loved us and given yourself
for us in Jesus Christ our Saviour.

22

Lord our God, help us to give our minds to you in our worship, so that
we may listen to what you have to say to us, and know your will.
Help us to give our hearts to you in our worship, so that we may really
want to do what you require from us.
Help us to give our strength to you in our worship, so that through us
your will may be done.
In the name of Jesus Christ our Lord.

23

Morning

Father, we praise you.
Your love never grows old: it is new with each new day.
This morning you are here shining through your creation, as you were
here at the dawn of time.
This morning you are here shining from the face of Jesus Christ,
showing us how to be properly human, promising life eternal.
This morning you are here as Holy Spirit in our hearts, making us

sorry for the sins we now remember, and for everything that has
gone wrong in the life of the world.
Come, Lord; bring in your kingdom. Establish your reign among us
here, and wherever your people meet. Speak, and let your servants
hear and obey.
Through Jesus Christ our Lord.

24

Sunday

To the great song of praise which rises to you, Father, from all the
world over this resurrection morning, we join our voices and our
hearts. May your Holy Spirit lead us in our prayers and help us to
look and to listen. Convince us of our sin, and of your forgiveness
for all who repent of their sin. May we have our share in the new
beginning you are offering to all mankind in Jesus, your Son. As we
seek to follow in his footsteps, may we be made more like him, until
at last we find ourselves fulfilled in your eternal presence.
Through the same Jesus Christ, our Lord.

25

Sunday

We praise you, heavenly Father, for all that reveals your glory.
Help us to look for you in all that we see, and to listen for you in all
that we hear.
Take from our lives everything that prevents us from seeing and hearing, blinding us to your presence and deafening us to the voice of
your commandment and promise.
We confess our selfishness of heart and meanness of spirit; our slow-
ness to forgive as we have been forgiven; our feeble resistance to the
upsurge of anger and the blandishments of greed.
Pardon us, Lord: set us free from our burden of sin and guilt. Sunday
is resurrection day, so raise us anew with Jesus into newness of life

and outlook. Let our hands be his hands, to do his work: let our
feet take the path he wills to tread in his world today.
We ask it in his name.

26

Sunday

Lord, on this first day of the week – day of creation, day of resurrection,
day of inspiration – receive the praises of your thankful people from
every land in every tongue. Direct our hearts to you in true worship,
and supply our needs: for the sake of Jesus Christ our Saviour.

27

At the Lord's Supper

Lord Jesus, once more in the midst of a busy life we gather to ask for
bread – strength to continue the journey, inspiration to call your
kingdom into being about us as we go.
We bring ordinary bread, but you make it special bread by sharing
your life with us as we break it together.
Help us also to carry the special into the ordinary. Let your presence
among us give point to everything we do.

28

Family worship

God our Father, we rejoice that you are our God all through our lives.
When we are tiny babies, you give us life and put us in families.
While we are growing up, you guide and protect us.
When we are fully grown, we still depend on your wisdom, power and
love.
When we become old, we commit ourselves into your hands.
We pray that you will draw out from each of us the love and service we
can give, according to our age and ability.

II
Confession

29

I will arise and go to my father, and say to him, 'Father, I have sinned,
   against heaven and in your sight, and am no more worthy to be
   called your child.'
In penitence we confess the many ways in which we have squandered
   our inheritance and imperilled our relationships, within our families
   and beyond them.
Have mercy upon us, our Father. Give to us, and to all who turn
   towards you in hope, the liberating assurance of sins forgiven. Mend
   what is broken. Continue towards completion your renewing work
   among men.
Lord, we come to ourselves when we come to you. We pray that you
   will so draw us to you that we may become truly ourselves, now and
   to all eternity.

30

Come, and let us return to the Lord.
Father, I have sinned against heaven and in your sight, and am no more
   worthy to be called your son or daughter: yet take me back into the
   service of your household.
Increase in my character and behaviour the fruits of faith and hope and
   love.
Let me no longer be conformed to this world, and to self-centred aims
   and expectations; but let me be transformed by the renewing of
   my mind, that I may leave self behind and take up daily the life of
   service.

May I be able to discern your will; to know what is good, and acceptable, and perfect; and to do it according to the pattern which Jesus has shown me, and in his strength.

31

Lord, it is when your praise is upon our lips and in our hearts that everything else begins to come straight.

It is then that we begin to see our problems and anxieties in perspective.

It is then that we begin to see things and people in their true colours.

When we think of you we realize that we are sinners, far from where we ought to be: yet sinners with hope of being forgiven. Father, let your Spirit within us turn us once again towards home. Grant that we may be more faithful members of your household and more serviceable subjects in your kingdom.

Through Jesus Christ our Lord.

32

Almighty God, our heavenly Father, you have made the heavens and the earth, and our help comes from you. We worship you as Holy Love, made known in Jesus Christ your Son. Take from our hearts everything that gets in the way of love, and everything that cheapens it.

We confess how blind we are. We have been afraid to ask you for our sight, in case we should see too well.

We confess how headstrong we are. We have not even wanted to know your will, let alone do it.

We confess the harm we have done, to other people and to ourselves, because of our ignorance and stubbornness.

Father, forgive us. Share with us the spirit and the mind of Jesus; and grant that his spirit may produce in our lives a harvest of love, joy, peace, patience, kindness, goodness, faithfulness, gentleness and self-control.

Through Jesus Christ our Lord.

33

Lord, you are not far from each one of us; for in you, our God, we live
and move and have our being.

Yet we do not always find you. Our minds are fogged by sin and our
wills are sapped by lies. The world dazzles and deludes us, making
us slaves to self, and doers of harm instead of good.

Lord, have mercy on us.

34

Father, in the presence of your glory we confess mankind's sin.

By our grasping and grabbing we have done our best to turn the world
you have given us into a desert.

Strong in ambition and mental achievement, we are yet too weak to
control the forces we have unleashed.

Capable of great vision, we behave like blind men stumbling in the
dark.

Constantly pouring out words, we have nothing to say.

Save us, Lord: help us. Let new hope spring forth for us from ancient
promise, and a way be found for mankind to return to you, through
Jesus Christ our Lord.

35

Father, you have done so much for the world that we cannot believe
you will give it up now. Yet before we can hope we have to share
with you our despair. Everywhere we look there are the ravages of
anger, resentment, injustice, cruelty and violence: and within, where
only we and you can see, Father, we walk the tightrope over a chasm
of potential catastrophe, the result of our failure to order our
energies and manage our conflicting impulses.

Yet your love never gives up. Once and for ever we have seen that there
is no limit beyond which you will not go to reclaim us and restore us
and re-create us.

Father, let us share your hope. Let your unflinching and unyielding
compassion lead us ever more surely into a new heart and mind, so
that we are transformed and can help in transforming the world.

36

God our heavenly Father, you are light and life to us. You have
promised never to leave us or forsake us: you are with us always, to
the end of the world.
All the same, things do come between us and you. Sometimes it is our
own fault, as when we are so full of our own virtue that we are no
longer looking in your direction, or when angry thoughts blot you
out. And sometimes it is not our fault, but the way the world is.
Chance often brings us some worry or sadness which fills our minds
so that everything is darkened.
Lord, when we are in the valley of that shadow, be with us still.
Even if we cannot see you, stay by us so that we never get lost. And
may your Holy Spirit show us day by day how we can better keep you
in view.
Through Jesus Christ our Lord.

37

In the presence of God who made us to be mirrors of his goodness, we
own up to our faults and failings. Especially to the fault of selfishness,
and our failure to love other people as much as we love ourselves.
This is how cruelty starts, and greed, and envy.
Father, help us to stop these things instead of starting them. Show us
ourselves as you see we are, and as you see we might be. Show us
our friends, and our enemies, as you see them. Show us Jesus, as our
brother in the world of time, and as your Son eternally. So may we
stand corrected by him and forgiven for his sake.

38

Lord, forgive us our sins:
    our sins against *faith* –
        for we have put our trust in material security;
        we have been afraid to make open profession of our faith;
        we have worried about being good enough instead of accepting
            your forgiveness;

our sins against *hope* –
   for we have forgotten how long the world had to wait for Jesus;
   we have despaired of ourselves and other people;
   we have dragged other people down into despondency;
our sins against *love* –
   for we have not loved you with all our heart;
   we have not loved our neighbour as ourselves;
   we have not let your love flood our hearts.
We believe that you have forgiven our sins.
Help us now not to dwell on them, but to approach today's life anew in
   faith, in hope and in love.

39

God our Father, as we join the worship of your people and remember
all your goodness to us, we are partly glad and partly ashamed. We
are glad because life is good and you are the giver of it. But we are
ashamed because the way we live is not good – certainly not good
enough. Sometimes we could not help ourselves: more often it was
our fault. Father, we need your forgiveness and the forgiveness of
many people to whom we have done wrong. We need your help to
overcome evil that is stronger than we are. These things we pray for
in the name of Jesus Christ, your Son, our Lord.

40

Lord, in the presence of your wisdom and love we confess our sins.
We have sinned against the light that is in us, finding ingenious excuses
   for not doing what we knew we ought to do, and for doing what we
   knew we ought not to do.
We have sinned against our neighbour, failing to value him and
   consider him as we do ourselves.
We have done much harm, and even our good is not good enough.
Father, all this is sin against you. We pray you to forgive us, and to
   recommission us in the name of Jesus Christ our Lord.

41

God of our salvation, our rescue, our health: all things are yours, and
when we bring our hearts and hands and voices to worship, we
bring you what is yours.

Yet we do not serve you as we should, and the world is racked by all
the tensions and outright conflicts which come from the worship of
that which is less than yourself. Our goodwill towards men has no
firm foundation, and crumbles at the first tremor of real testing. In
our personal affairs, and in our communal judgments, we try to heal
deep wounds with superficial cures.

Father, forgive us. Confront us with your way of righting wrong, your
strange work of redemption through the sacrificial love of Jesus. And
help us to love one another as he has loved us.

42

Lord, we pray for a better spirit.

We confess that we have been preoccupied with ourselves and have
turned a blind eye to the needs of others; that we have made promises
and broken them; and that we have hurt people through ill-temper
and spite or misjudged them through envy.

Have mercy on us.

Release us from the bondage of sin and guilt into the freedom of forgiven people.

43

Father, we confess that we are not as we seem to others, nor even as we
pretend to ourselves. You alone see us as we are: yet you do not
reject us. May the faith you have put in us cheer us into living our
lives more as you meant them and planned them. May your Son keep
working in us his miracle of transformation; and may the whole
world come to realize that it is yours.

Through Jesus Christ our Lord.

We confess that although there is but one Lord, one faith, one baptism, one God and Father of all, who is above all, and in all, and through all, men do not live in unity, at peace with God and one another. There is a driving force in each of us which is at loggerheads with the power of the Holy Spirit, distorting our good intentions, sometimes pushing them aside altogether, hustling us into doing the very evil we meant to avoid.

Lord, have mercy upon us . . .

Forgive our sins, transform us by the renewing of our minds, assure us that, in spite of all, you are not against us but for us. Speak to us now your healing word of grace, through Jesus Christ our Lord.

III

Our Response to the Promises

45

Lord God, to come to you is to come home, for you are eternally the
Father of all men. From you every family takes its name, and your
household of faith gives the pattern for every human household.
We thank you for showing us, in Jesus, that we belong to you and that
you care for us. Help us to believe it, and to believe that we ought not
to live so selfishly. Show us the deeper joy of service, and give us
pardon and peace through the Holy Spirit.
For Jesus Christ's sake.

46

We thank you, our Father, that through Jesus Christ your Son those
who seek you may find you. What you have made true for all we ask
you to make true in the experience of each. May all who set out on
the royal road come to the king's presence: through the same Jesus
Christ our Lord.

47

We sing to you because we are glad, our Father: and singing makes us
ever gladder. With joy in our hearts we give thanks to you for your
love which has given us life and the world, and your kindness which
stays with us even when we are ungrateful.
We have thought and said and done many things of which we are
ashamed, and more still of which we ought to be ashamed.

Help us to bring our lives into your light. Show us things as they
   really are, and take away our disguises and pretences; so that we may
   be open with you and open with one another – as you, Father, have
   opened your heart to all mankind in Jesus Christ our Lord.

48

Eternal God, our heavenly Father, we thank you for the mighty span
   of your love, reaching from the beginning of time to the end of time,
   broad and long, deep and high, setting free your creation to become
   what you mean it to be.
We do not yet see that liberation completed: but because of Jesus we
   are brought to the faith that it will be completed.
Let the assurance of your grace be a light of hope to us however black
   the shadows about our path.
And use us, Father, in the fulfilment of the vision you have granted to
   us.
Through Jesus Christ our Lord.

49

God our Father, your word renews our hope.
Help us to bring into the light of this hope all that seems to us most
   hopeless –
      the seemingly endless story of human atrocity;
      the seeming futility of so much human effort;
      the nightmare of physical pain and mental suffering;
      the apparent bleakness of the future of our planet;
      the seeming finality of death.

50

We are at peace with God and with one another through our Lord
   Jesus Christ.
Let us pray that the world may have peace – not any peace, at any price,

not unjust and compassionless peace, but this peace of the Lord
Jesus Christ, which the world cannot give to itself but must learn to
receive from him.

51

Lord, the words we hear from you are sometimes difficult for us to
understand: and what we think we do understand is sometimes even
more difficult for us to bear. We come to you loving life and thankful
for it; and you show us a cross, instrument of pain and execution.
Everything is too big for us – the world's need, your calling to us: we
cannot measure up to them.
Father, we are in your hands. Help us each day to do what you have
shown us of your will, believing that as we obey so we shall find
more of what is to be obeyed. Make your church, here and everywhere, a handier instrument of your grace.

52

Father, in words from the past we hear you speak to our hearts words
for today. We thank you that in Jesus Christ, who is the incarnation
of your purpose towards mankind, you are still causing hope to dawn
upon despair – still ousting darkness with light and death with life.
May this thankfulness of ours shape all our thoughts, all our words and
all our actions. May all the disciples of Jesus be light-bearers and
hope-bringers.
For his sake.

53

Lord, we pray that our thankfulness may always find expression in
obedience to your will; that our obedience may carry conviction to
others; that they in turn may come to know you, and to worship you
through Jesus Christ; and that so the chorus of thanksgiving may
swell and spread until the earth is full of the knowledge of your love,
as the waters cover the sea.

Let your Spirit keep us compassionate towards the needs we know, and
alert to perceive the needs you are waiting to show us. May none of
those who serve you lose patience or lose heart: but with our eyes
fixed on Jesus may we keep going in confidence, looking forward to
fulfilment of your plans and of our hopes through the love of the
same Jesus Christ our Lord.

54

Heavenly Father, we thank you for the fellowship which Christians
have. Near or far, we rejoice to be one family, sharing the same tasks
of ministry, disciples of one Lord.
May our membership of Christ's church always lead us to take a large
view and to accept a world-wide commitment.
Keep us sensitive to the presence and the prompting of your Holy
Spirit, whether he comes to us as conscience within, as the voice of
friend or neighbour, or as the pressure and logic of events. Your will
be done; your kingdom come: through Jesus Christ our Lord.

55

Lord God, we thank you for those who in ancient times longed that all
nations should know you and worship you, and for the solace and
support that the coming of Jesus brought them. We thank you that
the gospel is for all men.
Christian people have been wilfully blind, and have helped to erect and
perpetuate barriers of race and class and creed; and yet your church
remains a force to make men brothers.
Father, we pray that by your Spirit you will take what we are and what
we can be, and enable us to play our part in your purpose, so that in
this task we may be faithful servants of Jesus Christ our Lord.

56

Heavenly Father, we marvel and rejoice as we see the humble birth of
the child at Bethlehem lead to the world-conquering faith of saints

and martyrs – faith against which death and hell cannot prevail. We
thank you that again and again in the experience of Christians a seed
becomes a great tree.
Yet may we never forget what kind of conquest the conquest of faith
is. May we never, in confidence and enthusiasm, lose our humility.
Teach us, in all that we have to do, that your power comes to its full
strength in weakness, so that when we are weak, and while we are
still weak, then we are truly strong.
For Jesus Christ's sake.

57

Lord, it astonishes us that you, who are greater than all greatness,
should promise to make your home upon earth, and to inhabit the
fellowship of people like ourselves.
Be as good as your word.
Make us the instruments of your peace. Yet deliver us from merely
mouthing the words of peace. Let your Holy Spirit enable us to
penetrate deeply into the causes of strife and the secrets of reconciliation – both in those personal things nearest to us, and in the wider
public issues which confront and confound us.
Help us all to sort out our muddled ideals, and to work and live in
control of our lower natures. Where pity rises into anger, and anger
hardens into hatred, Lord protect us all. We do not ask you to take
our strength of will and feeling away, but to make it your own, lest
our efforts to help should turn bad into worse.
We bring this prayer in the name of our brother man whose pity and
indignation made for healing, not for destruction – Jesus Christ our
Lord.

58

Heavenly Father, by the ministry of your Son may we be drawn once
again into your purpose, incorporated once again into your pilgrim
people, strengthened for service.
Help Christians, in all the complications of obedience to your will, to

recognize when the voice of challenge or reassurance is that of the
Master and when it is that of the enemy.
Deliver us from using life's opportunities simply to nourish ourselves.
We pray now for those who are physically hungry, mentally hungry,
hungry for love, hungry to be treated as human. Lord, we see that
you may have to drive us into the desert sometimes to keep us sensitive. May we gladly endure limitation and hardship and fatigue if
it is going to help bring about the blossoming of your kingdom and
the breaking out of your streams of mercy.
Through Jesus Christ our Lord.

IV

Thanks

59

Father, we thank you for all the blessings of the life we share with the
whole company of mankind; and for the more abundant life into
which you are leading us through our faith in Jesus.

Help us to serve you in the daily duties of home and work, and in the
worship and fellowship of your church. May all our powers of body
and mind, our gifts of heart and hand and voice, be at the disposal of
your Holy Spirit and contribute to the making of your kingdom.

Through Jesus Christ our Lord.

60

We bless you, God our Father, for what you do for us. As the sun gives
light for our daily work, and leaves nobody out of its benediction, so
you give light for our inmost selves – light to live by, light to
choose by, light to rely on in the darkest times, light focused for us in
Jesus. With him, too, nobody is left out. He is a guide and a friend to
everyone who will turn to him, whether in the north or the south,
the east or the west. And we believe that it is your will, Father, that
all should be saved and come to the knowledge of the truth.

Have mercy upon your world, warped and twisted by the sins of pride
and greed, anger and envy, lust and laziness. Have mercy upon us,
and let your Spirit in our hearts win more victories over our besetting
sins. Give us strength to work for you while there is time: in the
name and for the sake of Jesus Christ our Lord.

61

Let us thank God for all his mercies.

Let us thank him for every sign of his presence and his love in our world, and especially for the power of truth to penetrate even men's blindness, and the insistence of love which finds a way into human hearts even in spite of men's deafness.

Wherever the lame man leaps up and the tongue of the dumb shouts aloud, this is your work, Father; and the man who brings these things about is your man.

We thank you for Jesus, and for his new way of holiness – away which discovers the beyond in the midst. Keep us pilgrims on that way – not refugees from the rough and tumble of the world but discoverers of the mystery at the heart of things – and help us at last to reach your presence, our home.

Through the same Jesus Christ our Lord.

(*Based on Isaiah 35*)

62

Father, we thank you for the thin-spun web of our life, slung so precariously between darkness and darkness. On it, like dewdrops glistening in the dawn, you hang bright jewels of awareness and yearning, of love and fulfilment – too great a burden of joy and wonder for such transience to bear. We praise you for Jesus, who shared the transience in order to give us new anchorage in eternity. Upon his inexhaustible strength we dare to see the destiny of the whole universe turn: in him our fragile dream becomes a sure and certain hope.

Father, help us again to find in Jesus our heart's true friend.

63

Lord, we thank you for the way our thoughts about you have changed since Jesus came into the world.

We said: No one can look upon God and live. But you are life.

We said: God dwells in thick darkness. But you are light and no dark-
ness at all.
We said: It is a fearful thing to fall into the hands of the living God. But
you are love, and perfect love casts out fear.
Because you are life we can live life to the full.
Because you are light, we can walk confidently, as in the light.
Because you are love, we are set free to love one another, as you have
loved us.

64

Father, we thank you for the company we enjoy as pilgrims on the
Christian road. We thank you for those who can tell how you rescued
them from wasting their lives, and for those who have a tale of
endurance or achievement in your name. Their cheerfulness shortens
the miles for us; their certainty makes us sure about our destination.
Help us in our turn to make the way easier for someone else, and to
draw all comers into our company.

65

Almighty God, our heavenly Father, we thank you for all the opportunities we have of sharing our faith with each other.
We thank you that we are not alone, that others whom we respect and
love are sure of the things we hope for and certain of the things none
of us can see.
We thank you that we in this church (*or* this school) are not alone,
that it is not only people of our generation, our country, our class,
our culture who believe, but a great number from every nation,
people and language.
Help us, in our exploring, to find out more and more what is worth
knowing, and enable us to express our faith and our gratitude in
deeds of love.

66

God our Father, we offer you thanks and praise for life and all its
blessings –
>the world of sight and sound, touch and taste and smell;
>the gift of language, the power to communicate with others and
>share our thoughts with them;
>the ties of family life and of friendship, in which giving and
>receiving become one and the same;
>the beacon of high ideals;
>and above all for the sense of eternal things amid all that changes,
>and for hope which dares to stretch out beyond the confines of
>this mortal life.

Father, all these things you give, but not everyone has all of them. In
the name of Jesus who went about doing good and making men and
women whole, we pray now for those who are blind or deaf or dumb.
For the paralysed in body, and the isolated in mind. For those who
have no one to trust, and who feel there is no one to trust and love
them. We pray for all whom force of circumstance condemns to
half-life: and for those also whose worst enemy is themselves.

All this we see, and yet there is so much we do not see.

Our prejudices distort our vision and make our judgments shallow.

Keep restoring our sight, so that we see people in their own right, and
not just for the good or harm they may do us.

Keep bringing us towards mature manhood – towards nothing less
than the stature of the fulness of Christ.

For his sake.

67

God our Father, we are yours. It is right that we should worship you,
for we are your own creation. Even if there were nothing else you
had done for us, we should owe you praise for this life you give us
and the wonder and beauty of the world we live in.

But there is more. You have stayed close to us all our lives. Sometimes
you have made yourself known to us in what other people are to us
or have done for us. Sometimes you have guided our actions by the

inner light of conscience and hope. Sometimes you have lifted us out
of worry or sadness by giving us in our hearts the knowledge that you
care for us.
We thank you, Father: and here in this fellowship of worship we own
up to the evil in us which has so often kept us from living as your
children. When we think of your love, and then of our anger and
greediness, we are ashamed; and we know that it is because of people
like us that there is so much unhappiness in the world. Have mercy
on us and forgive us. Bring us out of the slavery of evil into the
freedom and love which your Holy Spirit gives.
Through Jesus Christ our Lord.

68

Father,
    because of what we have seen, we have faith in what cannot be seen:
    because of what we have heard, we continue our journey in hope of
        a future beyond all telling or imagining.
Yet we should see and hear nothing unless you communicated yourself
    to us.
We thank you for your constantly renewed initiative to keep in touch,
    which we call your word:
        for Jesus, in whom this word was made flesh;
        for our forebears in the faith, in whom this word was a continuing
            reality;
        for the Bible which records and interprets so much of mankind's
            experience of this word;
        and for whatever is, for each one of us, the contemporary reality of
            your being and presence – the word which through Jesus,
            through the Bible, and through the fellowship, each one of us is
            receiving today.
Lord, since you are still in touch, may your word of command drive
    out the devils still and make your world whole. May we and all who
    confess the name of Jesus be brought ever deeper into your confid-
    ence and counsel. Let your word take human flesh still in lives which
    disclose your presence. Be, in the midst of human affairs, both the

giver of true peace and the disturber of false peace. Enable your
church to take the true measure of evil. Stop us from thinking to heal
the world's hurts with quack remedies. Strengthen us to struggle, to
suffer and to endure in the task of curing this great sickness.
We pray for those in whose hands lies power for good or ill. Help all
who work for justice to harness the energy your Spirit gives.
Finally we pray for those known to each of us who most need the help
and reassurance and renewal which your word enshrined in human
hearts can give. May there be people to minister your good news to
each of them, so meeting their needs and answering our prayers.
Through Jesus Christ our Lord.

69

Our heavenly Father,
   we thank you that
      because of the birth of your Son among us,
      because of the words of his lips and the light of his life,
      because of his willing sacrifice to the death and his glorious rising
      into power and majesty,
   we may be born again into newness of life.
May our thankfulness transform our whole outlook and behaviour,
through the power of the Holy Spirit.

70

Our God, we thank you that you are a Father who knows our needs and
supplies them, who knows our weaknesses and strengthens them.
Day by day your mercy sustains us. Day by day your forgiveness
liberates us.
Father, we thank you for all you have done for us, and we pray for the
accomplishment of all you have yet to do for us and in us.
Recall us from secondary preoccupations to the primary things: so that,
holding to Christ, we may be reconciled to one another and to life,
may find again meaning and hope, and so may win through to joy.
Through Jesus Christ our Lord.

71

Holy Father,
your thoughts are higher than our thoughts as heaven is higher than the
   earth. We are not in your class.
Yet you have made nothing of the difference. Instead of removing yourself from us, you have removed the barrier which stood between us
   and your presence. You have taken our transgressions as far away
   from us as the east is from the west.
This we know for certain because of Jesus. And because of him we
   know also that it is your purpose to break down all the barriers
   which divide men from one another, and to renew all that has become
   stale and corrupt, so that there may be a single new humanity in
   him.
Let Jesus be the world's peace. Let his holiness be a scourge to the
   complacent and a terror to the merciless. Let his compassion be
   strength to the weak and healing to the deranged in mind or body.
   Let his truth put to shame all the face-saving and all the time-serving
   of international politics. And let his dying love and risen power
   revolutionize men's ideas of what is great and worthwhile.
Father, your name is holy. Vindicate anew in our lives the holiness of
   your great name.
Through Jesus Christ our Lord.

72

We give thanks, God our Father, that we were not stopped on our way
   in to you. We give thanks for all the liberties we have inherited
   through the struggles and tenacity of those who went before: liberty to
   read the Bible for ourselves; liberty to worship where and how we
   would; and liberty to do these things without suffering any penalty.
   We can hardly imagine what it must be like not to have these liberties
   for oneself and one's children. Yet many are without them in today's
   world. Help us to cherish and extend them.
We give thanks above all, our Father, that you yourself do not keep us
   out – that you have accepted us alongside your ancient people Israel,
   making Jesus your Son the door of the sheep, through whom we may

enter your presence. We pray now for all who feel themselves excluded from fellowship – especially all those who feel shut off from you, by a sense of guilt or resentment, or for whatever reason. May no one ever be stopped by our pride or thoughtlessness from coming near to you. May our love be as all-inclusive as your own.

73

Lord Jesus Christ, we rejoice in your reign actualized and fulfilled in the world of men. We rejoice that people are finding freedom because you have freed them, life more abundant because you are alive. This is the truth, still hidden except to faith, which you have gathered us to celebrate and proclaim.

But as we do so, we see all too clearly the other half of the story – the part which everyone could see if he looked: race enslaving race, ideologies holding down ideas, human passions dictating human actions. Even your church is often aligned with injustice and oppression.

Lord of the church and of the world, we pray for both. We long for the more complete fulfilment of the vision you have given to us. We offer to you in this cause our God-given energies and abilities. May the Holy Spirit transform our minds, lest our efforts achieve the opposite of what we intend. And to your name be glory and thanksgiving for ever.

74

In this prayer, to the words, 'Praise our God!', the response is 'We praise him and thank him'.

Men and women, boys and girls,
    Praise our God!
    We praise him and thank him.

He is the greatest.
    Praise . . .

He cares for the smallest.
    Praise . . .

Because we are alive and have so much to enjoy,
    Praise . . .

Because his love makes even sad things bearable,
    Praise . . .

Through words written long ago and still true today,
  I Am, he says;
  You Are, we believe;
  He Is, we tell the world:
born once upon a time, but for ever at work among us;
killed once upon a cross, but for ever alive to help us.
    Praise . . .

We praise you and thank you, heavenly Father.
Tell us again the story of your love.
Through word and sacrament and daily work, make us part of the
    story of your love.
For the sake of Jesus Christ our Lord.

75

In this prayer, to the words, 'With all our hearts', the response is, ' We
thank you, our Father'.

God our Father, we thank you for the life you have given us here on
    earth. For the gifts of sight and sound, smell and taste and touch.
    For the power to think and to imagine, to remember the past and
    pray for the future:
    With all our hearts
    We thank you, our Father.

For ordinary days, and everything dear and familiar; and for special
    days and holidays, when enjoyment comes sharp and new:
        With all our hearts . . .

For the wonders of the universe, great and small – things shown to us
    by telescopes, and by magnifying-glasses and microscopes. And for
    the existence of other people like ourselves – our families and friends
    who make us feel at home in your world:
        With all our hearts . . .

For Jesus our Lord, who shows us that life's true happiness is in help-
    ing one another, and for the new hope which his kind of loving brings:
        With all our hearts . . .

We pray for the peoples of every nation, and for the church of Jesus in
    all countries: that through the lives and work of Christian men and
    women and children the voice of Jesus may be heard today above all
    the cries of hatred and anger and pride and pain. Your grace is able
    to do this, and therefore:
        With all our hearts . . .

And we pray for ourselves: that we, who have freely received so much,
    may be filled more and more with the Spirit of Jesus so that we give
    of ourselves for the sake of others. May your kingdom be made real
    in us because your will is done. And, Father, bring your great plan
    to completion, so that nothing that matters is lost, and all that you
    have made may glorify you and enjoy you for ever and ever.

76

Buildings

We thank you, Lord, that you have not created us to live alone. You
    have set the solitary in families, you have made it necessary for us
    to work together, you have given us pleasures to share. We thank
    you, too, for the chance to do things in pleasant and comfortable

surroundings. We thank you for homes that are warm and dry, work-places that are light and airy, concert halls where sound can be clearly heard, museums and galleries where the exhibits can be seen to advantage. We thank you also for the skill which has gone into the building of churches, so that they both make us aware of your presence and bring us face to face with our fellow Christians.

We do not imagine that you live in buildings made with hands. We know that people have encountered you under the starry sky, in the raging storm, in the peace of hillsides, in prison cells, in the faces of good people and in the cry of human need. We do not imagine that men can be converted only in a church. But time and again we have felt constrained to build, so that the newly awakened should not be dispersed, and that there should be room to worship and teach and congregate in your name.

Teach us, Lord, both to use our buildings and to be free from them, to your glory. Wherever your church meets, may its members always accept each other in mutual forbearance and love. And wherever you call your church to bear witness, may the opportunity be seen and gladly taken.

77

At the Lord's Supper

Father, we thank you for your good gifts. We thank you for a roof over our head, a bed to sleep in, a breakfast at the beginning of the day; our families, those whom we look after and those who look after us; the places where we work and where we learn; those who come to our rescue when we are ill or in trouble.

Forgive us that so often we forget that these are gifts and that we should be thankful. Forgive us for not sharing what we have as we might. Forgive the world for letting some grow rich while many more go hungry.

As we meet at your table, to break the bread which speaks of Jesus' sharing, and drink the wine which speaks of his life laid down for us, help us to absorb his spirit, and see the world through his eyes, so that what he came to do may be accomplished once again.

At the Lord's Supper

Heavenly Father, as we come to the gathering-place of thankfulness, we come with all your people. There is one bread, one body. Behind all differences of custom, all disagreement over this teaching or that, the people whose Lord is Christ are one people. Hallow us all to your service, and give us the love for one another which brothers ought to have.

Father, we come here not only with all those who name you, but with the vaster company still of all whom you have made, and who are yours whether they know it or not. They are here because we are here: for we are part of them, and they of us – our families, our neighbours, our colleagues at work, those whom we see on the screen and read about in the paper. We give thanks for them and pray for them. May the bread which feeds us here feed them also through us, our strengthened lives strengthening theirs.

Father, we find here the joyful and triumphant company of those who went before us in the faith – in their time stricken, like us, with difficulties, doubts, disasters, yet holding fast to Christ and so to thankfulness and hope. May we feel here the breadth and depth and strength of the foundations upon which our Christian discipleship is fastened. Give us in the fellowship of this table the pledge of our fulfilment in your eternal realms beyond time and death.

Through Jesus Christ, the source and guide and goal of all true prayer and all true life.

Mainly for Others

79

Lord, overcome our evil with your good.
Cover our sin with your mercy.
Meet our repentance with your renewal.
Come and re-possess the lives we ought never to have shut against you.

It is not only for our own sakes that we make this prayer, but also for
the world's sake.
May the fellowship of Christians in each place be such, in word and in
life, that people can recognize in it, with joy, an advance instalment
of what you have in store for all mankind if they will turn and believe.
We pray for the world's problems and needs . . .
And we pray for the sick heart of man – still, as it has always been,
capable of great heights but also of hideous depths. We pray for the
victims of anger and of calculated cruelty and brutality, and for all
passing through any kind of affliction . . . Use human sympathy and
kindness to bring home the reality of divine power and compassion,
so that the gracious Lord may be known through the gracious neighbour.
These prayers, and all the unspoken longings of our hearts, we bring
before you in the confidence of those who have heard their Master
say, 'The man who comes to me I will never turn away.'

80

God our Father, we thank you for the love which gave us life – heavenly
love made incarnate in the human love of parents.

We thank you for all the guidance for life and death which you give us
in Jesus Christ – a heavenly presence made known to us, often,
through earthly circumstances and companionships.
We pray for the groups and societies of men andwomen – families,
churches, cities, nations. We can see, and sometimes we can
also feel, that to these there come the same temptations that Jesus
felt – to satisfy their own hunger while leaving others unfed; to
take the wrong sort of risks for the sake of gaining reputation among
men; and to achieve power and mastery at the expense of that reverence for you which issues in humility and humanity.
We pray that we may learn from you how to resist these temptations;
how to put to constructive use the impulses and energies which our
circumstances call forth; how to win the fight against social evil and
disintegration without doing more harm than good.
Help us in all these things, Father, to take our cue from you just as we
have received our life from you, and to rejoice in your grace and
truth by honouring your commandments.
Through Jesus Christ our Lord.

81

God of love, we thank you for one another, and for all the wonderful
blessings you bring into our lives through other people – our families,
our friends, our teachers, our colleagues.
May we, in our turn, help to bring your blessing into their lives. And
in the world at large, too, may we recognize how much we depend on
one another. May people behave thankfully and humbly, not cruelly
or contemptuously.
Father, make known your power and your peace wherever men and
women are hard put to it because of decisions that must be taken or
pain that must be suffered, and wherever there is cause for great
anxiety or sorrow. May the grace of the Lord Jesus Christ bring to
them the assurance of your love: and may the church, the fellowship
of your Holy Spirit, be a comfort and a strength to them in their
trouble. May we prove ourselves to be the family circle of Jesus by

the way we carry out your will. And help us to make Jesus known as
Lord, by honouring him in our daily living as well as in our Sunday
speaking.
To him, with you, our Father, and the Holy Spirit, be glory for ever.

82

Father, we thank you that with the gift of your Son you provide for us
so much else – an example to live by; an anchor of hope in the midst
of darkness and storm; the spirit of love; the promise of life.
We pray that all over the world the church of your Son may possess
these gifts in abundance and may stretch them out to others. Where
impersonal forces rob men and women of justice and humanity,
give insight and realism and endless compassion to all who seek to
end the power of those forces. Where habits of violence rob men and
women of reason and mercy, keep alive in the leaders a vision and
sense of responsibility which will spur them to deal with causes as
well as with symptoms. And where accident, or deliberate injury,
illness, or old age, bring pain and terror or long vistas of distress, may
your love keep reaching out in the hands and voices of those who tend
and soothe and cure, so that even in the valley of deepest shadow
there is never lacking a life-saving light from heaven.
Father, it is Jesus who prompts us to form these prayers: it is in his
name that we offer them. And now we sum them up and seal them
in the words which are not ours but his.
Our Father . . .

83

Lord Jesus Christ, we believe that you are bread for all the world, the
very staff of life as it really is. And we understand that you have
given to believers the commission to be stewards of your sustenance,
to pass on the food of your Spirit.
Help us so to reflect on what faith means to us that we may be able to
speak of it in the language of common experience which others can
accept and assimilate.

In your name, Lord Jesus, we pray to the Father for all with whom life goes hard, and especially for such known and dear to us.

For all who are kept under by sin, or hounded by guilt.

For all who are in jobs too big for them.

For all who suffer because those who handle their destinies are callous, or crass.

May the Holy Spirit re-awaken men and women everywhere to that true self-respect which goes with a sense of responsibility. May we all come to realize how great is the love that you, the Father, have shown us – that we are called your children, and are not only called, but really are your children.

By the Spirit that makes that true for us, we are made bold to pray, on our own behalf and on mankind's,

Our Father . . .

84

Lord Jesus Christ, with you in the picture our vision of the world is transformed. You give new meaning to the familiar round of every-day things: new dimension to our decisions and opportunities: new hope in our failures and disappointments.

Grant that the gifts of your Spirit may equip us once again for the work of ministry in your world. Enable us to communicate and declare the visions you give us of the way things are. May the faith that impels us and the hope that draws us on meet in the here and now of love.

In love we pray for our fellow-pilgrims on the journey of life – especially for the discouraged; those who feel they will never make it; those who have no idea where they are going.

We pray for those who stand at a parting of ways and face some great decision; and for those who have taken some irrevocable step and have discovered that they have made a mistake.

Lord, may they all come to know you as the one into whose hands the book of anyone's life can be safely put. May they come to believe that you will read what is there with compassion, and accept it and take it with you into heavenly places.

85

God our Father, we pray for your church here and in every place.
Grant, as its hall-mark, confidence in the never-failing presence and
power of Jesus.
Preserve and renew day by day the life of your people, so that we all
may serve your purpose, whether in times of indifference or in times
of danger.
We pray for our nation, divided and uncertain, that in our political
choices we may each seek to put the good of all above any selfish
advantage. Rescue us from the spirit of envy which threatens to rule
our destiny. Give us instead a spirit of mutual service, and the courage to take the long view.
We pray for all who are passing through the ordeal of physical pain or
mental anxiety; for the victims of accident and terrorism; and for
those who bear the responsibility for the injury and death of others.
Finally, we pray for the dying and the bereaved; that in their time of
greatest testing their faith may hold, and they may know, in their
own experience, the consolations of the gospel and the fellowship of
all faithful souls in heaven and on earth.
In the name of Jesus Christ our Lord.

86

Let us pray for all who are learning in the school of suffering:
those who are ill, that they may recover health and strength, but also
that the time of weakness may not be wasted;
those who mourn the death of those near to them, that they may be
comforted, and learn to comfort others;
those who look after handicapped children, that they may have the
strength they need, and help to give meaning to lives that seem not
fully human;
those who are hungry or badly housed, that new chances may be
open to them, so that they can make the best of their lives;
those who are tempted to wrong ways of life, that they may hold
firmly to what is right and help to bring those who try to mislead
them to a new and better outlook.

87

We offer our prayer, Father, for all whose faith and character are being
tested now, by persecution or suffering, by moral temptation or
mental seduction. Help them to keep their eyes fixed on Jesus, on
whom faith depends from start to finish.

We offer our prayer for the world's leaders, as they seek to maintain or
to reconstruct peace. We pray that the hot blood of injured patriotism
may not overcome their better judgment and their vision of humanity
and its future.

We offer our prayer for the Christian church, here and in every place,
that however hard pressed by fears and doubts of many kinds, your
people may always remain receptive to your Spirit, ready to take the
next step in obedience and hope and joy, even when the further way
is obscure. Keep us all in the one communion of saints, companions
of the pilgrim way

Through Jesus Christ our Lord.

88

Father, we bring to you in prayer the hopes and the needs of mankind.
Each person you have made bears your image: but in each that image
is assaulted by many enemies. Hunger and homelessness, violence
and the fear of violence, greed, jealousy, boredom – all these threaten
the humanity of men and women which is your breath within them.

May your church everywhere be a force for peace with justice. May the
gospel of Jesus awaken everywhere such a vision of the real destiny
of man that evil may be overcome, not with other evil but with good.

And upon all who strive for the fulfilment of your reign on earth, may
there come such a spirit of trust and hope that nothing may seem too
hard to do in the name of your Son, Jesus Christ our Lord.

89

Prayer on the Jericho road

Lord, the wounds of the world are too deep for us to heal.

We have to bring men and women to you and ask you to look after

them – the sick in body and mind, the withered in spirit, the victims
  of greed and injustice, the prisoners of grief.
And yet, our Father, do not let our prayers excuse us from paying the
  price of compassion.
Make us generous with the resources you have entrusted to us.
Let your work of rescue be done in us and through us all.

90

Lord God, our heavenly Father, you call your disciples to many tasks
  in your field full of folk. Some to plant the seed you give them; some
  to water and tend; some to labour in a ready harvest. You are the
  one who gives the increase: and we pray for the growth of your kingdom in every land.
Especially we pray that your fellow-workers may not hold up the work
  by getting at cross-purposes with one another. May we spare no
  effort to make fast with bonds of peace the unity which your Spirit
  gives.
We pray for the world distraught, as ever, with violence and intrigue.
  Help us not to be driven to despair by our mistakes and lack of
  control. Teach men the gospel secret of reconciliation.
Finally, we pray for all whom darkness threatens to overwhelm. Those
  in the depths of pain or grief. Those bewildered or depressed. Those
  brought to their knees by the burdens of responsibility and decision.
Lord, receive our prayers. Make us members of the company of the
  living.
Through Jesus Christ our Saviour, who died to sin once, and lives to
  you for ever and ever.

91

Lord, it is not for escape from the demands of humanity that you
  rescue us from the island of our isolation. In the country of the soul
  to which you bring us, there are tasks both hard and long, battles
  against wrong whose magnitude we had not realized till you found
  us. Show your people day by day what they must do, and equip them
  to do it.

We pray for peace in a world of conflict and violence; for the peaceful
settling of grievances and injustices; for the peaceful resolving of
political differences and sectarian aspirations. Lay your powerful
hand of compassion and healing on innocent victims. Lord, wherever
we look there are things to frighten and horrify us. Help us to take
heart from your presence. Grant that however impenetrable the
darkness we may never lose hold of you. Help us all to live the best
we know, and in the end bring us all out of the dark into open sight
of your glory.
For Jesus Christ's sake.

92

Lord, we pray for light in our darkness: and in so doing we ask for
nothing less than an act of new creation on your part.
Yet even as we ask we know that our prayer is already answered: for
you have brought us to the confidence that when anyone is united
to Christ there *is* new creation.
And so we pray that what you have already done for man's salvation
may be known, and accepted, and lived out, by more and more
people. May each congregation of believers – may this congregation –
be enabled to reflect and pass on your light to others without
dimming it by laziness or lovelessness, and without distorting it by
extremism and conflict.
We pray that the light you have given in Jesus may shine renewingly
and reassuringly upon all who are passing through the valley of the
shadow of death –

> victims of accident or terrorism or natural disaster, their relatives,
> and all who are trying to help;
> those facing pain and uncertainty in hospital;
> those who know they must cross the river but don't know how to
> go;
> those who watch and wait and hold the hands of the dying.

Lord, upon all these may resurrection morning break in: and may each
one of us, with our different opportunities – and different difficulties –
go forward in faith and hope, knowing that nothing Jesus can call
his own is ever finally lost.

93

The versicle and response, 'Lord in your mercy/Hear our prayer', *may be used between the paragraphs of this prayer.*

Father, we pray that your whole church, in its ceaseless offering of worship, and its world-wide endeavours in the cause of truth and love, may lead all eyes towards the crucified and risen Saviour, and all hearts towards Christian faith and obedience.

We pray that as you loved the race that did not return your love, so individuals and communities may learn to love one another unconditionally and beyond deserving. May the gospel teach men everywhere, the leaders and the led, to transcend self-interest.

We pray for international relationships, community relationships, industrial relationships, family relationships. Renew, in the minds of all, the meaning of the one loaf broken for people to share.

Finally, we pray for those in special need of heavenly light and earthly support – the ill and the anxious, the persecuted and the deprived, the lonely and the unloved, the dying and the bereaved.

Receive these petitions and the petitions of your people everywhere. May the prayers of your church be points of access for you: and may the fellowship of heaven and earth, which you have made, and of which our worship is a pledge and foretaste, increase and endure to all eternity, through Jesus Christ our Lord.

94

God our Father, we thank you for our Lord Jesus Christ, who crowns all your other blessings to us, and makes sense of our lives.

As we pray before his cross, and invoke the everlasting mercy and compassion upon ourselves, our faith and hope reach out to our fellow men and women.

Remember for good your church, and all with whom your church makes common cause on human rights and on aid to the stricken.

Remember for good the leaders and legislators of this country. Deliver us all from selfish and sectarian interests. Let your spirit of peace and grace drive out prejudice and violence.

Remember for good all who are anxious and afraid; all who are impoverished by the falling value of money; all who feel that the worthwhile things are all crumbling away. Show them new gleams of hope and opportunities of good, and make our caring for one another's needs more of a reality.

Remember for good all who feel themselves outcast, and all whose agony is forgotten by the world because it does not happen to have hit the headlines.

Lord, in all these things you see the whole where we see only the part. We call upon your wisdom and your love. We enfold within the arms of prayer all whom we have named and all whose need is great. May the day come when pain shall be banished, illness conquered, and death itself put to death. Father, keep us now and to all eternity in the fellowship of the living.

Through Jesus Christ our Lord.

95

Father, when events alarm us we realize how fragile is the basis on which we build our lives. There is only one real foundation, Jesus Christ. Give us firmer conviction that whatever happens he will not be shaken.

We cannot forget that for some the nightmare of annihilation has come true while we were going about our ordinary ways. Some were killed in war; some on the roads. Some died of starvation. For them and for all who loved them we pray the assurance that in your eternal purpose it is not to nothing that we come when we die, but into the hands of your mercy.

We pray for the world's peace. For the United Nations Organization and all who serve it. For the statesmen who must bear all the strain of momentous decision, and all the burden of inside knowledge. For them, and for us all, may the measure of truth and hope and service be none other than Jesus. May all come to seek his light, and, seeking, find. May the time draw near when men make Christ's word their home, so that they know the truth and the truth sets them really free.

In his name and for his sake.

96

God our Father, we pray for the fulfilment of your purpose in Jesus,
that men should cease to live for themselves. Let the realization of
what he is for us spread wide and deep among the communities of
mankind. Let the church, called by his name, faithfully embody his
nature. Help each of us who are his disciples to see, each day, which
way we are bound to go for his sake.

We pray for the nations and their leaders: for the sorrowful and their
comforters: for the sick and those who would heal them: for the
dying and those who try to share with them and beside them a faith
in the things which are unseen and eternal.

Complete in each of us the new creation you have begun: and keep us
and all whom we love united to Christ, and so to one another in him
for ever.

97

Lord, we pray that your new order, already begun wherever your
gospel is heard and believed, may permeate and transform the old
order – that violence may be overthrown by peace, and ruthless
greed may give place to open-hearted service.

We pray for the humanizing of our economic systems; a fair deal for
the developing countries; the downfall of prejudice and unjust
discrimination; and the recognition of the sanctity of persons as
beings made in your image.

We pray for your church in all the world, and thank you for everything
which enables us to rejoice in its different parts and feel our oneness
with them. Help us to train effectively and deploy responsibly the
ministers and other leaders you give us.

Be known as strengthening presence to the ill, the lonely, the frightened
and the distressed. Be the God of our salvation – the God who makes
whole.

And to you, Father, Son and Holy Spirit, be ascribed the kingship and
the power and the glory for ever.

98

God our Father, we pray for all who take their stand for the truth as
they have seen it. Help them, and help us all, to be loyal without
becoming fanatical. May our enthusiasm always be at the service of
our love, and never the master of it.
We pray for those for whom faith is difficult – whether because of
persecution, or because too much has gone wrong for them, or for
any other reason. Through the help and friendliness of others,
keep before their eyes the steadfastness and simplicity of Jesus.
Father, recall our world to its senses. Heal the madness of those who
make everything and everyone the slaves of their own self-interest.
Wake us up to the reality of what life is all about: and let the city of
reconciled hearts ever grow and spread within the community of
mankind.
Through Jesus Christ our Lord.

99

To end an intercession

Within the horizon of our loving prayer we want to include all sorts
and conditions of men, all needs, all distresses. Yet we can know
only a fraction, and our thought is lost in the vast complexity. To you,
Father, ceaseless and unexhausted in your love, boundless in your
knowledge and care, we turn in confident hope, through Jesus
Christ our Lord.

100

Lord Jesus Christ,
We pray for your church – the inn for wounded travellers, to which you
keep bringing those whom you have rescued. Sometimes you give
special resources for new tasks: sometimes you throw us back on our
own resources. Help us to do what we can of what is needed, and
never to forget why we are here.

We pray for our suffering yet callous world – the world in which
news reports often add to the very evils they invite us to deplore;
the world of plenty in which so many are hungry; the world of
creative possibility in which so many are bored to the point of
violence.
Amid all the strident confusion of voices, Lord, may your voice be
heard in the deep places of the heart of man, recalling him to sanity,
to justice, to mercy and to peace.
And now, as those whom God has adopted as sons and daughters, we
gather up our spoken and unspoken prayers in the words you taught
us to say:
Our Father . . .

101

Father, we pray for your whole family of mankind.
For the household of the church, still keeping to separate rooms and
separate tables, meeting for odd moments on the landing. Help us
all to discover who in Christ's name we are.
We pray for all who struggle for peace with justice, both in political
fields and in the fields of economics and industry. And we pray for
those who must bear the brunt of suffering as long as solutions fail.
We pray for the ill, the handicapped and all who endure the mental and
physical frustrations of old age. May the touch of the living Lord
work in them miracles of hope: and may we learn to use wisely for
them every resource of body and spirit that you have given.
We pray for all who stand on the brink of their death, and for whom the
night is dark. Like Stephen may they look up and see a rift in the
cloud and the light of your eternal glory in the face of Jesus Christ.

102

Heavenly Father, let your power for good be known through those who
have your Spirit. Let your light break in on human blindness and
your summons on human deafness. May those whose lives are
crippled by pain or disappointment, by handicap or breakdown, by

lack of opportunity or lack of recognition, learn and experience that
inward healing, that peace of the soul, which the cures of Jesus can
bring about even in the midst of this uncertain world.

And, Father, as you bring your kingdom near already, so bring us all
to its fulfilment in the eternal world.

Through Jesus Christ our Lord, to whom, with you and with the Holy
Spirit, be the glory and the praise for ever and ever.

103

Father of peace, God of truth and love, we thank you that you have
never been one to say one thing and do another. You have fulfilled all
your promises in Jesus. He is for us the way, the truth and life.

Make your people doers of the word as well as hearers of it, so that the
house you are building for yourself among us may not crumble.

Recall the world of men and women to your commandments of love—
love towards you and love towards neighbour. Guide to yourself
the groping of those who seek to enhance their perception by experi-
menting with drugs or dabbling in the occult. Conquer the fears and
make up the inadequacies which cause us to attack one another and
delight in inflicting injury.

We pray for all who are in the loneliness of pain or the desolation of
bereavement. Lord, lighten their darkness and let grace break in
upon bitterness and hope upon despair.

We walk by faith, our Father. We see the promises, but sometimes
their fulfilment seems very far off. May the company of your people,
both here on earth and ahead of us in heaven, comfort and encourage
each one of us as we go, till by your mercy we also attain to blessed-
ness, and live with you for ever.

104

Almighty God, Lord of all, we pray that the Spirit of Jesus may bring
faith and hope and love to all mankind.

We pray for the church, the company of believers through whom Jesus
can make his power and mercy known and available to men and

women today. We pray that our discipleship may make our Master known, not hide him from view.

We pray for the world's leaders – those few who take decisions upon which the state of life of millions depends. Especially we pray for our own government and opposition, that concern for the common interest and long-term good may prevail over the pursuit of sectional advantage or short-term solutions.

We pray for peace in the world – peace based on a just distribution of rights and commodities. We dare to hope for what seems utterly unlikely – that among the peoples of mankind love will overcome greed and pity will overcome heartlessness. Give wisdom from above, and grace which reflects your own grace.

We pray for all who are handicapped, whether from birth or because of disease or accident. May the infirmity of others always bring out the best in us and not the worst. Let your Spirit conquer fear in us and despair in them.

We pray for all in any kind of crisis or distress. Be with them, Father, to steady and to strengthen.

Finally, we pray for ourselves, that our prayers may never be an excuse for postponing the action we can take. Lord, live in us, so that what we do may be your work, through Jesus Christ our Lord.

105

Lord God, when we remember your unvarying goodness towards us our own doubts and sorrows seem less important. We pray that all who are passing through a time of trouble may receive the confidence that is your gift. Where man can help directly, let the right hand of human sympathy and neighbourliness hold up the stumbling and nerve the frightened. And let the knowledge of your love bring a dawning hope even to those who feel that all is lost.

We pray for the nations of the world and for our own nation. In a day of new economic alignments among the rich, do not let the needs of the starving go unheeded. In a land where freedom is taken for granted, do not let us dismiss as none of our business the plight of the victims of tyranny. In a world whose history is written in battles

and conquests and rebellions, teach us how to make peace, and how
to live at peace without getting bored.
We pray for the whole church of Christ. Give joy and strength to your
people as they work out their faith in worship and service. May our
leaders have the confidence and humility which are needed together
if Christians are to be helped towards maturity rather than kept in
spiritual infancy. Give us all vision and grace to make you known in
life as in word: and unite us in faith, hope and love with all who have
run the great race before us and finished the course.
And now, with Christians of every tradition and language, in the
fellowship of the Holy Spirit and for the salvation of the world, let
us pray the Lord's Prayer.
Our Father . . .

106

Heavenly Father, we come seeking your blessing on those who are
dear to us, and those whose needs are close to our hearts. You know
our longing for them: but you know also, better than we, what is
really best for each one of them. Give what you have to give: and if
sometimes to us the priorities seem the wrong way round, and we
want to say, 'Not that, Lord, but this!', bless and enlighten us as
well.
We pray for all who are astray in life and who yearn for the seeking and
saving love of a reliable shepherd. Make it appear that you are their
Saviour and mighty Deliverer.
We pray for all who are trying to give good gifts to those who depend
on them – gifts of leadership and advice, gifts of affection and compassion. Deliver them from the sore temptation to attach strings to
their charity, and to try to run the lives of those they would lead and
help.
We pray for the household of faith, and especially for the churches of
this area. In what we do together, help us to be faithful in proclaiming the truth about your love: and in what we still do separately,
deepen our commitment to the one Lord of us all, Jesus Christ, our
Saviour in time and for eternity.

107

In this prayer, to the words, 'Lord, in your mercy', *the response is,* 'Hear our prayer'.

Heavenly Father, we praise you for the knowledge that men are meant to be like you – made in your image, and commanded to reflect your limitless goodness. Have mercy upon us who fall so far short, and hear us as we pray for the fulfilment of your good purpose for all the world.

That the races of mankind may learn to live together as brothers:
> Lord, in your mercy
> *Hear our prayer.*

That we may recognize and combat in our own society the prejudices and injustices that we deplore in others:
> Lord . . .

That Christians may use to the full the gifts of imagination and compassion which you give, lest our presentation and living out of the gospel truth about man should fail to connect with the modern mind:
> Lord . . .

That the way of love may be evident not only in our wide concerns and general pronouncements, but in the hard particulars of our ordinary personal dealings, morning, noon and night:
> Lord . . .

For all our dear ones, wherever they may be; all who bear the burden of pain, or grief, or difficult decision; all whose public smile hides private agony; and all who slept hungry or homeless last night:
> Lord . . .

108

Heavenly Father, Lord of space and time, lifter up of men's eyes to far horizons: we celebrate before you in worship the courage and skill which you have given to human beings, enabling them to journey to the moon or cross oceans in rowing-boats. Glory be to you for the spirit of adventure which is in man, and in which we all have part.

We only wish we could achieve as much on crowded land as in the empty spaces of sea and sky. It seems that to cope with our fellow men is too much for us. Wherever we look we see war, terrorism, the clash of economic interest; the double-talk of the rich, and the resentment and desperation of the poor.

And if we look within, to our own mixed motives, we see the same picture of conflict and frustration.

Lord, as well as showing us the far horizons, give us a more compelling vision of your plan for the world on our doorstep and in our hearts. May Jesus, whose name is both Son of God and Son of Man, be more and more the pattern for men's dealings with one another, so that we may cease trying to overcome evil with evil and learn how to overcome evil with good. Father, it is your world: teach us all how better to align ourselves with your way of righting wrong in it.

We pray for our fellow Christians, and for all who stretch out in longing towards the highest, however they name it. Sustain and correct our sense of values. Help us to show in life what we believe in heart and mind. Give us hope, the child of faith, and love, the fulfilment of hope. Let your grace come to its full strength in our weakness.

Through Jesus Christ our Lord.

109

We give you thanks, God our Father, for your life present among men in Jesus Christ, and in the Holy Spirit which is yours and his. We thank you for your transcendent power shown wherever heavenly treasure is found contained in human earthenware. Sometimes we glimpse in one another your sublime strength manifest in apparent weakness. Sometimes we are able to see that even in the failure of human plans and the death of human hopes the frontiers of your kingdom of love are being extended.

As we give thanks, we pray that your whole church may more faithfully reflect your splendour, and more completely be transfigured into your likeness. Renew the minds of all your people, so that they may be enabled to share creatively your baptism and your cup – the pain of identification with others, of compassion and sacrifice, of willing servitude, of 'love to the loveless shown that they may lovely be'.

We pray for all who make decisions – especially for those whose choices are a matter of life and death to others, or make the difference between prosperity and hardship. Spur us to seek out more effective ways of making known, in the corridors of power, the controversy you have with earthly standards of government and ordinary conceptions of authority. And may our personal lives confirm what our public endeavours promote.

We pray for all whom we love, especially for those in any kind of trouble. By the patience of hope keep them and us united in the fellowship of holy things; and bring us all at last to completeness in Jesus Christ our Lord.

110

A minister's prayer

Lord, you have made me a minister to people who are already your own.

You love them, you have taught them, you have led them.

In times of crisis they will draw especially on the resources you have already given them.

Help me to support them in the ways I can,
>   neither imagining that I am their only helper and trying to do too much,
>   nor making unfamiliar situations and protracted problems excuses for giving up too soon.

Help them to balance the claims of home and work, church and community life as they should.

Do not let them feel guilty when they cannot do as much in the church as they would like,

but do not let them cut themselves off too easily.

May they find as much satisfaction in our corporate work as in their personal achievement.

VI
Contemplating Jesus

III

Lord Jesus Christ, we give thanks and rejoice that we belong to you.
  We are yours; you are our Good Shepherd; no one can snatch us
  from your care.
    Through you we draw near to the Father.
    Through you we receive the gift of eternal life and a share in the
      Holy Spirit.
Help us to worship you in your risen power.
Help us to rely on your forgiving us for our sins and accepting us in our
  unworthiness.
Help us to be to one another what you are to us.

112

In Christ, dear friends, all our need is fulfilled.
    Would you be healed? Christ is the healer.
    Are you weighed down by your sins? It is he who clears you.
    Are you in need of help? It is he who comes to your aid.
    Has night overtaken you? Christ is the light.
    Are you lost? He is the way.
    Would you be delivered from lies? Christ is the truth.
    Are you afraid of death? Christ is life.
Happy is the man who puts his trust in him.

(*Translated from 'Cinq Projets de Liturgie' of the Reformed Church of
France*)

113

Why do I praise Jesus Christ?

Because he is the best that man can be, and because he makes known to me what God thinks about me, and how I ought to think about God.

I praise him because when he lived on earth there was love in everything he said and did, and because in my heart God shows me that love is right and good.

So if I follow Jesus I am living in the way my heavenly Father means me to live. But I praise him also because when I fail to follow him he does not turn me away, but forgives me and puts me right and goes on loving me whatever happens.

When I praise Jesus Christ I become part of a huge crowd, far too great to count, who are praising him too. Everyone here belongs to that great company: so I belong with everyone here. Young and old together, we are his servants. We have the same Lord; and together we pray our Lord's prayer.

Our Father . . .

114

Let us remember Jesus' compassionate searching for the outcasts of society, and pray for a like compassion;

Let us remember his renunciation of home and family for the sake of the kingdom of God, and pray that we too may desire to do God's will above all things;

Let us remember Jesus' conflict with the powers of evil, and pray for the same courage to stand against what is wrong;

Let us remember his refusal to be bound by old tradition, and pray that we may use this freedom for ourselves and concede it to others;

Let us remember the way he fulfilled his people's hopes, and pray that we may mediate his love and power to our own time;

Let us remember his words of judgment on his own nation, and pray that our nation may not reject what he stands for.

(Based on C. H. Dodd, 'History and the Gospel', ch. 3)

115

O God, in the days when Jesus lived on earth, he summoned men and women to follow him. We still feel his words as a summons to us. And yet we do not find it simple to follow him. The modern world is very different from Palestine two thousand years ago. And we are not completely free agents. We have responsibilities to our families and to the community at large. We cannot leave all and follow him just like that.

Teach us to obey within the family, to follow as good parents, good brothers and sisters, good husbands and wives, good children. Help us to accept life's restrictions and to obey in the ways that are open to us. Yet make us ready to break with any loyalty that cripples our loyalty to you.

We are people of our time, but we are also people who know Jesus, the crucified and risen Lord. We are called, as others have been in the past, to accept the power and guidance of your Son. We believe that he strides through our time as purposefully as he preached and healed in Galilee and set his face to go to Jerusalem. We believe that he sends us out, as he sent out the first apostles, with the resources to accomplish his will. Help us to see the adventures to which his living spirit beckons us. May we have the courage and the persistence to make friends and forgive enemies, to bring strangers together, to serve and suffer in his name.

Lord, we hear Jesus' call to follow him in breaking down barriers of race and class. We hear his call to follow him in freeing those who are in bondage to disease and fear and habit. We hear his call to follow him in seeking unity with all our fellow Christians. Help us to respond to his call.

116

In this prayer, to the words, 'Lord, in your mercy', *the response is,* 'Hear our prayer'.

Let us think about Jesus, our Master and Lord, and so make our prayer.

'He came not to be served but to serve, and to give his life as a ransom
   for many . . .'
Forgive us, Lord, that we have not better followed in your footsteps.
   Help us to stop trying to shape everything to our own advantage and
   convenience.
      Lord, in your mercy
      Hear our prayer.

'He came that we might have life, and have it in all its fulness . . .'
Show us, Lord, the worthwhileness of life when it is lived for you.
      Lord . . .

'He went about doing good, and healing those who had been wounded
   by the power of evil . . .'
Sometimes we know our need of his healing touch. But let us also ask
   that he will come to us in those other times when we need him but
   do not know it.
Lord, I am not worthy that you should come under my roof: but say
   the word, and your servant will be healed.
      Lord . . .

Receive our prayers and the prayers of your people all over the world.
   Set our feet once again on the road to heaven. And show us that along
   that road lies also the kingdom of heaven upon earth.
For your own name's sake.

   117

Father, we thank you for the splendour of your eternal light coming
   into our world in Jesus, so that you are hidden no more, but visible
   to mortal man.
We praise you for the glory of the revelation in the face of Jesus – a
   glory seen not only at the obviously glorious moments, but also in
   the common things of life, and even in the pain and degradation of
   death: glory as of the only-begotten of the Father, full of grace and
   truth.

In the kindness and constancy of a man we have seen the kindness and
constancy of God. May our lives so catch and reflect the light of this
revelation that we may be changed into the same likeness ourselves,
and thereby help to spread the shining of your light before men.
And to you, our Father in heaven, may the glory be given by us and by
all men, for ever and ever.

Heavenly Father, we thank you that when you came among men in the
person of Jesus of Nazareth you came as a member of a human family,
with lineage and descent. You came not lone and terrible, sweeping
ordinary things aside, but as part of the family firm: and so, in the
name of Jesus, we can pray about the ordinary things of life, confident that they are part of your care.
We think of Jesus as son of Joseph and Mary, the carpenter and his
wife, and pray for all workers and craftsmen and those who employ
them. May service be rewarded by trust, and trust in its turn lead to
treatment that is humane and just, so that society may be a community of concern and not merely the convenience of the rich.
We think of Jesus as cousin of John the Baptist, and pray for all upon
whose faithfulness the true word of prophecy depends for a voice
today. Bless your church here and in every place; and let us never
become so concerned with church affairs that we lose sight of what
we are here for.
We think of Jesus as descendant of David, and pray for all who need
a shepherd to keep them from the precipice, all who need a king to
set confusion in order, all who are slaves to something too powerful
for them and need a giant-killer. Lord, be strong for them and be
gentle with them: lead them in right paths for your name's sake.
We think of Jesus as descendant of Ruth the Moabitess – an immigrant
alien among the chosen people – and we pray for racial harmony and
for world peace. May the Lord who is the man for all persuade all
men to realize their brotherhood in him.
Lastly we think of Jesus as descendant of Adam – which is to say, 'of
Man'. We thank you that he thinks nothing human to be alien to

him, and we pray for the accomplishing of that marvellous and universal purpose whereby, being lifted up, he is drawing all men to himself.

119

Lord Jesus, as you still come to us, an eternal presence walking upon the moving waters of time, help us to recognize your approach and come to you. Give us the faith and the courage to do things your way, even in these storm-tossed days when so many cry out for security or vengeance, or keep their mouths shut when they should speak. Help your people to be done with the old motivations, the sad, sin-scarred reactions of which we say, 'After all, it's only human nature, isn't it?' Let your Spirit lift us on to new levels of vision and forgiveness and trust, so that your church may show the world once again what it really means to be human.

In your name who are for ever Man of Nazareth and Son of the Living God, Jesus Christ our Lord.

120

Lord Jesus, your majesty amazed those who witnessed it; and we are amazed. We are amazed on the mountain, where your majesty is seen in a vision of glory: we are more amazed still in the valley below, where your majesty is seen in the authority of your conquest of evil. There you give us an example: it is for your people to follow you today in overcoming evil with good.

We pray, Lord, do your own work in and through your church. Human need is so vast that we are daunted by the burden. Yet there are many who belong to the Way, and each of us has different gifts for you to use in some part of your healing and redeeming task. So first of all help us to promise our best: then hold us to our promise when the moment comes.

For your own name's sake.

121

We have seen strange things today – strange and wonderful things,
  things to fill us with awe, things for which we give glory to God.
Divine power made manifest in human weakness we have seen: eternity
  shut in a span: God making his dwelling among men and speaking
  to the likes of us as a man speaks to his friend.
For sins forgiven and hope renewed, when we had no power of ourselves to help ourselves or to storm heaven by force of character,
  we give glory to God, through Jesus Christ our Lord.

122

Lord Jesus Christ, you know what it is like to be human, yet you
  managed not to let pride and anger get the better of you: you were
  not greedy for power or praise. Touch our hearts with your Spirit, so
  that we may become like you. Give us grace that we may show grace
  in all our dealings. May all that you came to begin on earth be fulfilled.

123

Lord, it is difficult for us to pray that you will unsettle us. We spent so
  long looking for peace of mind and security of tenure. We keep
  thinking that at last we are beginning to know where we are. Then
  you come again and turn everything upside down. A Jew among Jews,
  you portray yourself as a Samaritan; you heal Gentiles; you sit down
  at table with the lowest of the low. Wherever you go, you upset our
  ideas of a fair reward, and you overturn our flourishing livelihoods.
So we know that if we would be your disciples we must try to pray
  that you will unsettle us. Rouse us again to be a pilgrim people,
  seekers of that which is not yet.
Nevertheless, though we look for a city and a kingdom not of this
  world, do not let our search take us away from the world. It is not
  only that we may come at last to your kingdom that we pray,
  but that your kingdom may come at last on earth. Therefore help

us to bear in thought and word and deed day by day some part of the burden of the world's redemption. Keep alive in us an active sympathy with the victims of misfortune, injustice and war. Give us grace and strength in our time to untangle some of the knots that history has tied in human affairs. May all that we do and say and are make for life and not death, respect for the other man and not contempt.

For your name's sake.

124

Let us give thanks to God for the testimony of Christians to Christ, and for all the words of scripture that become for us parables of him. Often our hearts have burned within us as he talked with us by the way: the miracle has become familiar. Let us pray God to renew it for us now, and to renew our wonder as his Spirit speaks once more to our spirits the things concerning Jesus.

125

Lord Jesus, merciful and faithful high priest of mankind: you are able to bring us into God's presence, for in you we find that God's presence has come near to us.

We pray your help for all who are passing through personal crisis – of health or of affairs, of self-respect or of family accord. Steady them upon your example; grant them your Spirit.

And may we and our fellow-Christians be found ready to help minister your companionship for the lonely, your healing to the sick, your provision for the hungry, and your hope for the dying.

126

Lord Jesus, if once we have come to the conclusion that you are God's promised one, the world's redeemer, we are no longer free men and women. The demands of your love are all about us, constraining us to turn from ways of selfishness to ways of service.

Help us now to take up once again the ministry of reconciliation which
is committed to us by the Father who was in you.

By your Spirit re-create your church from within, so that the life of
your people in the world may make it easier, and not more difficult,
for men and women to believe in a God of love.

Show each of us day by day the ways in which you would have us turn
private religion into public commitment. Son of David, let the
weapons of your humility and service kill in us and through us the
dread giant of pride and self-sufficiency. Reign in the hearts of all
who long for you. May the prisoners of despair be freed, and the
mourners take heart. Glory to you for ever.

127

The love of Christ constrains us.

Constraint is not all keeping in.

If we say that we feel constrained to speak at a meeting, we mean that
we feel impelled – pushed out.

The love of Christ constrains us in this way too.

It pushes us out into the world like babies being born.

Through the gospel we gain new life, become part of a new order.

So here is a paradox – that the love of Christ deprives us of freedom, yet
gives it to us; limits our choice, yet pushes us out into an uncharted
territory of new choices.

I love my Master, I will not go free. Yet in this service I shall find
freedom.

128

We pray for the Spirit of Jesus.

May his example inspire men and women to rise to the true height of
their humanity in serving one another's interests and not only their
own.

May his pity shame us out of our callousness.

May his humility shame us out of our pride.

May his welcome shame us out of our rejections and antagonisms.
Lord, may your living Word, made flesh, speak to the heart and mind of
man today.

129

Lord Jesus Christ, we give thanks that when you came among men you
both fulfilled and confounded their expectations.
They were looking for a king, and as a king you came: but king of love,
wearing the likeness of a slave.
Fulfil our longings still, not as we in our ignorance have formed them
in our minds, but as you know them most deeply and truly to be.
We ask it for your name's sake.

130

We thank you, God our Father, that you have always loved the world
you made. We cannot believe, as men have sometimes believed, that
perhaps you have changed your mind about mankind, and may
change it again. If we hear this from the stories of the past we shall
know that people could only have thought it because they had not
seen Jesus. He is the proof of your great love towards the race of men,
even though we were sinners: and in you there is no variation, no
play of passing shadows of mood or intention.
We thank you, Father, with all our heart that we do not have to wonder
about this any more or worry about it. You are for us: who can be
against us? Nothing can separate us from your love. Nothing can
separate us finally from anyone who shares your love. Lord, we
praise you for the victory over fear which you are passing on to us
through Jesus Christ our Lord.

131

Christ crucified

O God, we thank you that on the cross Jesus' kingship was proclaimed
in Hebrew, Greek and Latin:

We believe it should still be proclaimed to every man in every language;
Help us to make it known by the way we talk and by the way we live.

132

The road to Emmaus

Lord Jesus, you helped your disciples to see recent events in a new
light. You helped them to understand that the crucifixion had a
place in God's purpose. We too are sometimes shattered by the
brutal and sordid things that happen in our world. Help us to believe
that it is still worth living and suffering for what is right and that no
sacrifice will be in vain. Grant your courage to those who are
oppressed and the patience to work and wait for the day of deliver-
ance.

Lord Jesus, you showed your disciples how to find light and truth in
ancient scriptures. In them you found direction for your own life,
and you used them to encourage others. Help us, as we search the
scriptures, to draw deeply from their wisdom and let their teaching
penetrate our hearts.

Lord Jesus, you showed yourself to the disciples at the supper table.
You promised to be with disciples wherever two or three of them
meet in your name. Open our eyes to your presence, not only on the
expected occasions in church, but also when we meet as families at
home and when we entertain guests. Let no one miss you, Lord.
Come to unite men and women, boys and girls, in wonder and faith.

VII
Offering

133

Father, by the help of your Holy Spirit may giving and sharing be the
pattern of our lives, as it was the pattern of the life of your Son our
Saviour Jesus Christ.

134

Heavenly Father, bless our giving.
Since it is your love that enables us to give, may it be your love that is
known through the gifts.
In the name of Jesus Christ our Lord.

135

Lord, our lives are yours. May our daily work reflect our worship here,
and may we offer in your service the best of all that you have given.

136

Lord, in our giving we pray
that all your people's love
may be your kingdom's gain.

137

God our Father, may your Spirit, who moves us to give, take hold of
all that mankind offers you in worship and obedience, and make of it
the fabric of your kingdom and your city.
Through Jesus Christ our Lord.

138

Lord, by this offering we commend into your hands the life you have
given us. All things are yours, and you are the source of all good to
us and your whole world. May we so abide in you that your life-
giving Spirit may flow in our lives and bring us to fruition.

139

Lord, by the offering of money, which is power, we mean to submit to
your control all the strengths you have given us. So may we and all
that is ours be useful to your purpose among men, through Jesus
Christ our Lord.

140

Father, in presenting these gifts for the work of your kingdom we know
well that your richest blessings are those which money cannot buy –
joy and peace in believing. So do not let us simply give our money and
leave it at that: but may our outward actions express our inner will
to make our whole lives an offering, dedicated, fit for your acceptance
and use.
Through Jesus Christ our Lord.

141

Father, we dedicate these gifts to you in hope – a hope which begins
here and now, yet stretches further than human eye can see.
Show us, we pray, how our own behaviour day by day may give your

caring love more scope. May our divided minds be more and more
absorbed in your single purpose, so that we may cease to live for
ourselves and live for him who for our sake died and was raised to
life – Jesus Christ our Lord.

142

Almighty Lord, we believe your word in Jesus Christ is for all men.
It is a word which all men need – as our own hearts would tell us
even if the news we hear did not.
What you have shown, let the lives and interactions of your people also
show, so that reconciliation may be credible because it is manifest.

143

Father, receive the dedication of our gifts; enable us to offer ourselves
to you, a living sacrifice; and so by your grace make us part of the
story of your redemption of the world through your Son, Jesus
Christ our Lord.

144

Lord, take our willingness to give as a measure of our eagerness to
receive your gift. Let your love find a way in the world through the
things you have entrusted to us.

145

Lord God, may the money we bring be both a prayer and a promise:
a prayer to you to make the gospel live in today's world through the
work of your church; and a promise from us that we will try to play
our part faithfully.

146

Father, our gifts are part of our thankfulness. You do not need them for
yourself. But you need them for men and women made in your image.
May we see you and serve you in them, and may they find you in us.
For Jesus Christ's sake.

147

God our Father, in your hands is the outcome of everything. What you
ask of us is not that we should solve every problem, but that we
should do our own part in your world as faithfully as we can.
Receive us now with our gifts: confirm us in the faith that Jesus is
Lord: and grant us always the help of your Holy Spirit, for Jesus'
sake.

148

Since every act of giving is a kind of small death; since every opening of
our hands betokens in some sort a world lost to ourselves; Father,
may we find in losing, and live by dying, today and every day, because we belong to Jesus Christ our Lord.

149

With heart and hand and voice give thanks to God!
We were lost and he found us.
We were prisoners to self and he freed us.
We were tossed to and fro and he steadied us and set us up upon a
rock.
Our heavenly Father, with our gifts we rejoice before you; and we pray
that through the proclaiming of your grace many may come to believe,
so that still greater may be the chorus of praise that ascends to your
throne, through Jesus Christ our Lord.

150

Beyond our understanding, Lord, almost beyond belief, are the ways
of your love with us. Through all that threatens our faith, all that
clouds our hope, and all that hinders and distorts our love, help us to
keep our eyes on you. May our hearts give thanks to you and our
hands serve you, that God may be glorified in you. We ask it in your
name.

151

King of the world, Lord of our lives: in deed as in word we would
acknowledge your sovereignty over every realm of life.
Come, Lord Jesus, enter into your kingdom. Let the victory remain with
love.
We ask it for the sake of your name above every name.

152

Gifts for the work of the church

Father, be with us in our offering and also in our decision-making, so
that our love and support for the church may be found to be love
and service to the world.

153

In church

Lord, by this offering we make our prayer, that we may be ever at the
service of your church, and your church ever at the service of your
world.
Through Jesus Christ your Son.

154

In church

Lord, may this offering be more than a collection of money to keep an institution going. Take the dedication of bodies and minds and use us to fulfil your purpose in the gift of Christ your Son.

155

In church

Heavenly Father, may our gifts, of time and money and love, help to sustain your church at home and abroad. And may your church proclaim and manifest your kingdom, so that men everywhere may know you and be reconciled to you, and the world may find its true peace in Jesus Christ our Lord.

156

In church

Father, in Jesus you have shown that the ordinary things of life, when turned to obedience to you, can be the means whereby you make known your presence. Give us in this offering, and in the use your church makes of it, that inward obedience of the heart which can make our life together the pledge that Jesus reigns.

157

Gifts for special need

Lord Jesus Christ, you have promised to accept the serving of your brothers and sisters as service to yourself. Receive in these gifts to the hungry and the stricken our praise and prayer. To you, our Friend and Redeemer, with the Father in majesty and the Holy Spirit in perpetual benefaction, be ascribed all glory and blessing for ever.

At Christmas

Help us, Father, like shepherds and wise men of old to lay our gifts of
hand and heart at the feet of your Son, and to put our lives at his
disposal in the service of the kingdom of heaven upon earth.

159

At the Lord's Supper

Lord, may these gifts of money and bread and wine, which represent
our livelihood, serve your purposes of good. May we use them in the
spirit of Jesus and towards the coming of his kingdom.

160

At the Lord's Supper

Father, you have made it so that in simple actions of giving and sharing,
and simple things like money and bread and wine, we can express our
highest beliefs and deepest loyalties. May it be so now. We put this
moment of dedication into your hands, asking you to take it, and to
minister through it your gifts to men of peace and renewal: through
Jesus Christ our Lord.

161

At the Lord's Supper

Lord Jesus, by a marvel of grace you take what we in our poverty can
offer and make it the means of your presence in glory. Accept the
money and bread and wine which we have brought together on your

table. Gather us and our gifts into your purpose. Nourish your world with the love you evoke. We ask it in your name.

162

At the Lord's Supper

Heavenly Father, as you have given us the resources from which to supply this table, help us to give in thankfulness and in hope. May what we provide, in worship and fellowship and obedience, be a means by which you are recognized in the world, through your Son Jesus Christ our Lord.

163

Gifts of money at the Lord's Supper

Freely we have received: freely we should give.
Father, as these gifts of money have been taken up, and carried and laid on the holy table next to the symbols of your presence and love, so may each one of us be willing to move out from known comforts and settled ways, and make the journey of self-giving towards the fulfilment of your gracious plan.
Through Jesus Christ our Lord.

164

At the close of worship

Here we stand, Father, ready to go. May all our going be at your behest, all our arriving be in your name. May the gifts you have committed to us return to honour you; and may all that we are become filled with your Being.
Through Jesus Christ our Lord.

At the close of worship

Lord God, we leave with you something of our livelihood, something
of ourselves – a pledge of our intention to serve you every day and
with all we have.
So too may we take with us a pledge of yourself – the Holy Spirit in our
hearts, an ever-renewed vision of Jesus Christ in glory, your light
for life and for death and for eternity.

VIII

Short Prayers on Single Subjects

166

Love for God

What shall I render to the Lord for all his bounty to me?
I will reverence him as my creator.
I will not forget that he has made me in his image.
I will give him the service that is his due as my master, the love which
  is his due as my father.
I will be honest about my sins.
I will put myself out for those he has made my brothers.
I will be loyal to my fellow members in the church (*or*, the school).
I will try as a friend to understand his purpose.
I will help him in his work.
I will welcome him into every part of my life.
I want to be like him, and to share his eternal life.

(*Adapted from 'The Life that is Light'*)

167

Friends

Let us pray for our friends, that they may lead happy and useful
  lives;
Let us pray for any friends with whom we have quarrelled, that we
  may have the chance to be reconciled;
Let us pray for those who are living in new surroundings, and lack
  friends;

Let us pray for those who have lost their friends by the way they
    live;
Let us pray for those who befriend the friendless.
God our Father, make us true and loyal friends. Grant that all our
    friendships may lead us nearer you.

168

Faith in God

God our Father, help us to believe in Jesus Christ and give him our
    allegiance despite the obstacles to faith that there are today. We
    wonder how things that happened so long ago and so far away can
    be important to us. Old arguments have lost their force for us.
    Many around us have turned away. But where else can we go?
    No one else has the secret. And Jesus really does remake people's
    lives and reconcile them to each other. We know that blindness and
    laziness and sinful reluctance contribute to our unbelief. We expect
    too much from faith, wanting it to make everything crystal clear and
    free from frustration. Save us from our illusions, and give us a steady,
    mature faith that gives our life its true direction.

169

Those who doubt

Father, we pray for those who are seeking faith:
    for students and others searching for a pattern of life which will
        neither stifle nor corrupt them;
    for those who have ceased to expect anything radically good from
        life;
    for those who are crushed by the daily struggle with poverty or
        sickness or by the demands of others.
It is here that the Christian faith has been so powerful in the past.

May the story of Christ and the love of Christians bring renewed life
and hope to many people.

170

Forgiveness

O God, you have not dealt with us according to our sins, nor rewarded
us according to our iniquities: help us not to presume upon forgiveness by living carelessly, nor to disbelieve it and be weighed down
by guilt.

171

The church

Lord, help your church in every country to be one, overcoming the
barriers of church tradition and theological suspicion;
holy, obeying your commands and resisting temptation;
catholic, having an identity which is more important than social,
political and racial divisions;
apostolic, witnessing for you as the first disciples did.

172

Other people

God our Father, as we pray for other people we remember that in some
things we are all alike, with the same needs
for security and freedom, for the love of other people and your love;
and in some things we are different, having different abilities, different interests, different backgrounds and different opportunities.
Help us to despise no man, remembering all we have in common, and
to misunderstand no man, respecting the differences between us.

173

The next generation

Lord God, our heavenly Father, as we praise you for your goodness to
us, we pray for your help in making you known to the next generation. We do not want to indoctrinate them, so that they cannot but
think as we think. But as we give them freedom to explore and choose
for themselves, help us to give a good account of our faith, both in
what we say and in the way we live. May theirs be no second-hand
faith, but true and direct discipleship. Help them to see your will
more plainly than we have seen it, and give us the humility to learn
from their fresh vision.

174

Freedom

Almighty God, we thank you for the liberties this country enjoys, and
for those who have worked and suffered and fought to secure them:
for freedom from war and want;
for freedom of thought, conscience and speech;
for freedom of worship.
Give us grace to defend these liberties and to use them responsibly in
your service; and grant that they may become the secure possession
of all men – everywhere in the world.

(Based on Franklin D. Roosevelt's 'Four Freedoms' speech, 1942)

175

Freedom

Let us identify ourselves today with those who are not free from the
grip of poverty, who work hard for little reward, who have large
families and have to watch them starve, who are ignorant or suspici-
ous of birth control – let us pray for the hour of their release.

Let us identify ourselves with those who are not free to express their
  convictions, who must keep silent or run grave risks, who are
  detained or imprisoned – let us pray for the hour of their release.
Let us identify ourselves with those who are not free to be educated or
  to take the jobs they are fitted for or to travel, because of the colour
  of their skin – let us pray for the hour of their release.
Let us identify ourselves with those who are not free from the terrors of
  war or civil strife – let us pray for the hour of their release.
Let us identify ourselves with those who are not free from the power of
  sin or fear or unbelief, who have not been set free by Christ – let us
  pray for the hour of their release.
Almighty God, our heavenly Father, set the earth and its peoples
  free from all that makes life poor and degraded and disgusting.
  May all men attain their true dignity in serving you. May no man
  seek to prove himself free by taking away the liberty of another.

176

The nations

Almighty God, you have created a great variety of nations and peoples,
  each with its own language, customs and way of life:
  may this not be a cause of suspicion and strife, but lead to the enrich-
  ment of our life in this world.

177

International co-operation

We ask your help, Lord God, for those nations who have joined in
  common enterprises.
We pray that the barriers of language may be overcome, and that mutual
  understanding and trust may grow.
We pray that barriers created by national pride may come down, and
  that the gifts and abilities of other nations may be welcomed.

And we pray that new barriers may not be set up against the rest of the
world, but that the spirit of co-operation may extend to include all
men.

178

The peace of the world

We who have known war thank you, God, for the blessing of peace.
May this be extended to every part of the world, and be built securely
on goodwill, fair dealing, patience and restraint. May the years of
peace not be squandered in selfish living, but be used in the pursuit of
justice and truth.

179

Reconciliation

O God, you have taught us that we should return good for evil, not
evil for good, nor even evil for evil: show us how this can be done by
nations and groups, as well as by individual men and women.

180

Nations at war

We pray, Lord God, for the nations which are at war:
    that the fighting may end as soon as possible;
    that statesmen may not cease to think how a just peace can be made;
    and that even in the stress and anguish of war men and women may
        not lose their humanity, but show mercy to their enemies and
        keep their word.

181

Racial harmony

Lord, though the roots of racial conflict lie deep in our history, help us
to outgrow attitudes which are irrational and wrong. Enable us to
see that no man is despised, or made poor, or denied opportunity,
because of his race or colour; and give us the courage to champion
the rights of others, even though this draws hostility on ourselves.

182

Racial harmony

Lord, strengthen the hands of those who work to draw together people
of different races.
May the children who play together remain friendly as they grow older.
May students enter deeply into each other's worlds.
May those who live as neighbours or work together strive to create
truly human bonds.

183

Social order

Keep us alert, Lord our God, to the changes of our time and their
effect on the lives of men and women. Help us to welcome and promote the reforms that will benefit them, and to support them through
times of hardship. And help us to accept change in our own lives
without resentment and without fear.

184

Social order

We pray, Lord,
for those who rebel against the present order of society, openly or in
their hearts;

for those who can find no work;
for those denied opportunities because of colour or creed;
for young people repelled by the values of their elders;
for working people dissatisfied with conditions or pay.
Help us to see the justice in the protests of others, and to answer their
cry.

185

Social order

Lord, make us quick to understand your will and to recognize the need
of others,
and ready to support what is right before it becomes popular;
so that we do what we can willingly and at once,
not grudgingly and out of fear.

186

Justice

Lord God, we believe that you love to see justice done between men.
Help us therefore to strive after justice in all our dealings:
to pass fair judgment, to speak the truth and to pay what we owe.
And when today's conditions make yesterday's justice unfair,
enable us to think out afresh what is required of us.

187

Justice

O God, we recall your condemnation of those who take bribes: help
those who administer justice to be scrupulously fair, and show us
all where we let favouritism or prejudice prevent us from being
completely just.

188

Justice

O God, we remember that you have said that workmen deserve their
wages: help us to see that all by whose labour we benefit, in this
country and in every part of the world, receive a fair return for their
work.

189

Our country

We pray, Lord, that the nation to which we belong may live by the light
you have given and honour and obey your laws.
We pray that all sections of the nation may enjoy equal rights and
opportunities, and that we may impoverish none by driving prices
and wages too high.
We pray that we may conserve the resources of the earth, and share the
benefits they bring more equally with other nations.
In our dealings with other countries, may we be neither self-righteous
nor timid, as far as possible living at peace with all and doing what is
right in the sight of all.

190

Good government

Almighty God, our heavenly Father, we give you thanks for the blessings of good government. We thank you that we can walk about the
streets unmolested, that no one stopped us coming in here, that we
are free to follow our chosen way of life. We thank you that we have
been born into a peaceable country and that those who enforce our
laws are courteous and patient. Help us to appreciate these your
gifts, to honour those you have put in authority over us, and to hand
on these liberties to the generation to come.

191

Industry

We pray, Lord, for the industries on which so much of our livelihood
    depends:
  that what is produced may be good, and pride be taken in it;
  that the way work is organized may foster self-respect and good
    personal relations;
  that the environment may be respected and the earth's resources not
    be wasted.

192

Industry

We pray, Lord, that in our industries there may be peace and not
    strife; that both management and labour may accept the need for
    change, and plan to make it and meet it together.

193

Those who live in the country

We pray, Lord, for all who live and work in our countryside. May they
    not feel cut off from the main stream of life, nor have their way of life
    destroyed by the encroachment of the towns.

194

Farmers

We remember, with gratitude, Father, the work of farmers in all parts
    of the world who provide our daily food. May they all receive a fair
    return for their labour. May their methods treat both animals and
    the soil with care. May they be spared the effects of disease and bad
    weather.

195

Harvest

We pray, Lord, that the earth may yield its full harvest again this year, and that we may distribute it wisely and fairly, so that all your children may share in it according to their need.

196

Reverence for life and nature

Teach us, Lord, reverence for all the living things with which we share this earth. Help us to respect their right to life and to spare their habitat wherever possible, to take life only when we must, and to inflict no cruelty.

197

Seafarers

We pray for those who put to sea in ships large and small. Defend them in bad weather; save them from loneliness and boredom; and watch over their family life.

198

Daily work

Lord, help us in our daily work:
    to master difficult tasks calling for skill and patience and insight;
    to be of service both to our firms and organizations and to our customers and clients;
    and to make what contribution we can to the peace and health of business and industry.

199

Office workers

We pray, Lord, for men and women busy about their daily work:
for those who are taking big decisions, that they may do what they
are convinced is right;
for those who are meeting others in conference or committee, that
they may speak frankly and temperately to each other;
for those who are dictating letters, that they may give careful and
helpful replies;
for those who are answering the telephone, that they may be courteous and painstaking.
May the world be better for the work done today.

200

Daily work

Let us pray for people in their daily work:
those about to leave school, that they may find work they are fitted to
do;
those who have been put out of work or whose jobs are threatened,
that they may soon find new work;
those whose work carries the danger of accident or disease, that
nothing needed for their safety may be neglected;
those whose jobs are boring or dirty or badly paid, that their conditions may be improved;
those who feel discouraged, because they have not achieved what
they wanted to achieve, that they may know that faithfulness is
more important than success;
those who work alone, at home or without colleagues, that they may
have the stimulation of company in their leisure.
Lord, guide and strengthen us in our work day by day, so that we may
have no cause to be ashamed of it.

201

Daily life

Lord our God, you are in every place, and every place where you are is
holy ground. Fill our hearts with wonder and joy as we journey along
the ordinary paths of life: so that in them we may catch sight of you,
and, seeing, may adore your presence and serve your purpose.
Through Jesus Christ our Lord.

202

Man in community

Lord, you have given to each of us an identity to cherish and rejoice
in. We thank you for that uniqueness which is ourself. Yet you have
made us all of a kind, and you bring us to our true maturity through
relationships with others. Help us to trust you enough to give ourselves away in love: and in that death of self may we find life and
lasting fulfilment, following in the steps of Jesus Christ our Lord.

203

Sincerity

Help us, Lord, to be the same people in public and in private. Help us
to be genuinely interested in people, genuinely friendly, genuinely
devout, genuinely zealous. Help us to practise what we preach, and
to preach nothing we are not prepared to practise.

204

Testing times

Lord, we cannot tell in advance what strains and dangers we shall have
to face for your sake. We cannot be brave beforehand. But may our
longing to be loyal to you prevail over our fears, so that when the
testing time comes we may not let you down.

205

Refugees

We pray, Lord, for all those who have been forced to leave home and
country. We pray that as many as possible may find a new home,
work that satisfies them and a country they can love. And for those
who remain in refugee camps, we pray that there may yet be hope of
a new and worthwhile life.

206

Human need

Remember, O Lord, the basic needs of every man and in your mercy
supply them:
the need for food, that every man in every country may have enough
to eat;
the need for health, that medical skill and adequate nursing may be
within the reach of all who require them;
the need for justice, that no one may be denied his fundamental
human rights;
the need for peace, that all men may have the chance to live without
war or the threat of war;
the need for the knowledge of God, that your reality may come home
to our generation and your purpose be followed.

207

Non-Christians

We pray, Lord, for those who are not Christians, asking that we may
share our faith with them, for we believe that no life can be complete
without faith in you. Help us to say what is helpful at the right time,
and to live considerately, leaving the outcome in your hands.

Non-Christians

We pray, Father, for those who are not Christians but share some of
our ideals: those who on humanist grounds care about social justice
and personal freedom, world peace and racial harmony. We believe
that men cannot achieve these things unaided, without a new spirit.
We ask that as we join with these people in common enterprises,
and discuss our faith with them, we may all appreciate the power of
Christ afresh.

209

Non-Christians

O God, we read that those who give Christ's disciples a cup of cold
water shall not lose their reward: help us to appreciate the goodness
of people and the goodwill they show, even when they do not belong
to the church.

210

A better world

Set before us, O Lord, a vision of the world we can create, directed by
your wisdom, urged on by your Spirit:
  a world in which we treat our fellows with tolerance and respect,
  however different from ourselves they may be;
  a world whose resources we gladly share with each other and with
  the generations to come;
  a world in which every sign of your presence is eagerly sought and
  reverently prized.
May no difficulty sap our faith or extinguish our hope that we can live
together in peace and love.

211

A better world

Let us share with God our hopes for mankind:
> that every person born into the world may have the chance to live a full and healthy life, with enough to eat, a sound education, work to do, freedom from war, tyranny and injustice;
> that every person may be awake to the reality of God, and respond to the call of Christ;
> that where suffering does exist, people may be quick to help each other and able to surmount handicaps;
> that our life may be enriched by the contributions of writers and musicians, painters and sculptors, and entertainers of every kind;
> that the church may be found helpful by increasing numbers of people.

212

People of other religions or beliefs

Lord God, in a world where there are many different religions and beliefs, save us from two errors:
> from thinking that there is no ultimate truth;
> and from supposing that we have that truth whole and entire, and that others have glimpsed nothing of you.

213

People of other religions or beliefs

Father, help us who have been brought up as Christians and to believe in Christianity as the true faith
> to recognize men and women of other religions as our fellow human beings, to respect their convictions, to learn from them all we can,
> yet still to remember they are people for whom Christ died.

214

People of other religions or beliefs

We pray, Father, for the adherents of other faiths.
We do not really understand how beliefs about ultimate things can be
    so diverse.
Help them to see what we have seen,
    and help us to see what they have seen,
    so that all our faiths may be fully tested through their contact with
    a wider world.

215

Walking by faith

Although we cannot see, we believe.
Although we cannot see, we love.
Unknown God, be known to us in Christ,
    and in our sharing of the search.

216

The indwelling God

Father, our life is yours: may your life be ours. Through Jesus Christ
    our Lord.

217

The indwelling God

Lord, may your church more and more embody your purpose. May
    we and all your people be receptive to your light and responsive to
    your command, that the fellowship of faith may be in deed as well
    as in name the instrument of your kingdom.

We pray for the world so full of need, so short of real compassion. Father, only your life alive in men can overcome the dark powers of greed and fear. Do not leave us to our fate.

218

The rewards of God's service

We thank you, Lord God, that your service is so rewarding. We serve one who cares what we make of our lives. When we do wrong, we feel that we have not just broken a rule but failed a person, and we welcome every sign of your discipline and reproof. When we do well, we feel that we have delighted you, and given you back something you can use in your purpose. You do not make us rich by this world's standards, but you reward us in so many ways, through friendship, through the growth of other people in character and insight, through the society of the church, through the privilege of belonging to Christ. We praise you through him.

219

The rewards of God's service

O God, you have taught us that those who do good to gain approval from other people have their reward already: teach us to do good without drawing attention to ourselves, and to be content that good has been done, even if others get the credit.

220

True wealth

Help us, O God, to take to heart what we are taught in your word about true wealth.
Help us to store up our treasure, not on earth, but in heaven;
to avoid that love of money which is the root of all evil things;
to be content with what we have.

You endow us richly with all things to enjoy:
grant that we may prize what is true, what is noble, what is just and
pure, what is lovable and gracious;
that, having seen the pearl of very special value, we may desire it
above everything else, and gladly give all that we have to get it;
that we may count everything sheer loss if only we may know Christ
and find ourselves united with him.
Let us become rich in your sight:
rich in faith, and able to bring wealth to many others.

221

The word of God

Let us thank God for revealing himself to our world, and for sending
the church to proclaim the gospel of Christ to every creature.
Let us thank God for the disciples who went two by two to proclaim
the coming of the kingdom; for the apostles who carried the gospel
throughout the Roman Empire and beyond; for the unknown missionaries who brought Christianity to these islands.
Let us thank God for those who founded the great missionary societies;
for all who have left home and country to live and work overseas;
for missionaries and converts who have suffered through their faith
in Christ.
Let us thank God that the church now praises him in every country
and in every language.

222

Before reading scripture

O God, as we turn again to the gospels and the record of Jesus' life on
earth, help us to understand the kind of person he was and all that
he has done for our world.

223

The word of God

We pray, Lord, that you will prosper the work of the Bible Societies,
and increase the support they receive.
We pray that those who translate the scriptures may produce versions
which are accurate, clear and a pleasure to read.
We pray that editors, printers and binders may so present the Bible
that people want to handle it and possess it and turn to it again and
again.
We pray for those who distribute the scriptures, that they may be
alert to all opportunities presented by bookshops, newspapers and
radio.
We pray that those who comment on Bible passages may make plain
what is obscure and bring home the message to heart and conscience.

224

Right use of the scriptures

We thank you, God our Father, for the recorded words of Jesus:
    for those heartening words which have taught men to trust you as
        their Father;
    for those demanding words which call us to leave everything else to
        follow him;
    and for those sharp words of warning and reproof.
May his words search our consciences, strengthen our faith and confirm us in our discipleship.

225

For the mind of Christ

Lord, help us to learn, from one another and from Jesus, how to be
confident without being arrogant; how to be sensitive without being
overwhelmed; how to fulfil the mission which our one Lord has
laid upon us all.

226

After reading scripture

Lord our God, our hearts rejoice to hear once again the words of eternal
life, the message of your love which never comes to an end, which
could face even the cross for our sakes, and which is stronger than
death itself. We thank you for all the blessings of our life on earth,
and above all for the chance to love and the experience of being loved
which you have given in different ways to each of us. Though sometimes love brings pain almost past bearing, it carries us to the very
centre of the meaning of life – the heart of your reality. We thank
you for this precious gift from your own heart, made known to us
in Jesus Christ our Lord.

227

After reading scripture

Lord, we thank you for the testimony which has come to us down the
ages with renewing power through your church.
We thank you for the chance you still give us in Jesus your Son to live
in the way you always intended us to live.
You have made him for us not only an example but a living helper and
friend. As we try to walk closer to him we see better where we ought
to go; and we gain strength to overcome temptations and take a
different path.
Have pity on our efforts; make us more worthy of the name of 'Christian'; and give us joy in our Lord now and always, for his sake.

228

After reading scripture

God our Father, we bless you that your work in the world throughout
history has been the same – the work of love, and of drawing all
men to yourself.

May we so receive your eternal word that the gift of faith is stirred to
   flame within us.
Through Jesus Christ our Lord.

   229

After communion

Lord, we have heard great things today – better things than the newspapers have to tell. We have received again, for ourselves and on
   behalf of all the world, your promise of forgiveness and renewal, of
   salvation to the uttermost even for those beyond human hope.
Father, as at the family table you have taken us into your confidence,
   meeting us in your Son and playing host to all our needs, so grant
   that now, in our daily encounters, we may be hospitable to one
   another, for your Son's sake, Jesus Christ our Lord.

IX

Longer Meditations

Worship

Eternal Wisdom, eternal Power, how can we speak as if we knew you? How can we behave as if we were treading familiar ground? If you made the universe on such a scale and living things in such profusion, how can we begin to conceive what you are like? If you design the minutest living creature down to the last molecule with such care, how can we imagine we are sensitive to your mind? What is our maturity against your eternity? What significance can our work possibly have?

We should despair if we did not believe that you have made yourself known and unfolded your purpose for us. You sent your servants the prophets to arouse and enlarge the conscience of mankind. You did not withhold your Son, your only Son, from us. You have teased men into giving the best of their thought to the study of your ways and your nature. You have made people uneasy and restless until they devoted their lives to declaring your love for sinful men and women. You have constrained yet others into the fight against evil and for the realization of good.

Forgive us that the Christian response has not always been of this quality. Forgive us that we have often been content to worship an idol of our own making, neither the maker of all things nor the father who cares for the least of his creatures. Forgive us for thinking of your service in an inadequate and stereotyped way. Remember that we are men, who cannot always realize the ideal nor even keep it steadily in view. Remember the care you have taken with us, the

love you have shown us. Do not let us fail or come short of your
purpose for us.

Three ways from a single starting-point: I John 3.1.

I

See what love the Father has given us, that we should be called the
children of God.
By his own wish he made us his sons and daughters through the Word
of truth, so that we might be a sort of advance instalment of his new
creation.
Heavenly Father, we are thankful to know that we belong to your
family: but we must admit that we do not always live as if your father-
hood mattered to us. We have failed to do things we knew you wanted
us to do: sometimes we have actually gone against your will.
Father, we have sinned, against heaven and in your sight, and we are
no longer fit to be called your children.
Yet in the greatness of your love, we pray, receive us again into your
family circle. Help us to worship you in spirit and in truth. Help us
to live more nearly as we pray.
Through Jesus Christ our Lord.

II

See what love the Father has given us, that we should be called the
children of God.
See what commandment the Son has laid upon us, that we should love
one another as he has loved us.
See what wonders are wrought by the holy and life-giving Spirit, who
day by day makes even our poor obedience fulfil his plan, so that we
carry about in the body the dying of the Lord Jesus, and exhibit,
however faintly, the marks of the kingdom of heaven.
Lord God, Father, Son and Holy Spirit, we pray that you will bring
your purpose to fulfilment through the children of your promise. To
you be glory for ever.

See what love the Father has given us, that we should be called the
children of God: and if children, then heirs – heirs of God and
joint-heirs with Christ.

Praise be to' the God and Father of our Lord Jesus Christ, who in his
mercy has given us new birth into a living hope by the resurrection
of Jesus Christ from the dead.

Praise be that the inheritance to which we are born is one which nothing
can destroy or spoil or wither.

Praise be that even already, to those with eyes to see, 'earth's crammed
with heaven, and every common bush afire with God'.

Father, we pray that we may continue to have, day by day, those intima-
tions of your presence by which our faith is fed. And we pray that
your church may so faithfully interpret to the rest of mankind the
meaning of things, that the number of those who believe may continually increase.

We pray that wherever it is gathered in fellowship your church may be
alive with your life. May those who are just beginning to wake up to
your reality find among Christians what they need to bring them to
firm conviction.

Father, in the light of your Son Jesus reveal yourself to all people
through their ideals and strivings, and through the needs of their
fellow men. Be a shield to the vulnerable, and strength to the weak.
Bless the peacemakers, and heal the wounds of war. Restore to the
double-minded and unstable their lost integrity. Uphold those who
suffer pain, and those who must watch others suffer. Do not let
anything in life or death, in things present or things to come, separate your children from the knowledge of your love, as it is in Jesus
Christ our Lord.

232

The whole armour of God – I

Lord, we pray that you will equip us for the warfare against evil.

Help us to know our enemy. Save us from hating and destroying fellow
human beings. Enable us to identify those forces which lead us into
sin:
wars which turn neighbours into enemies;
economic crises which make us selfish;
rapid changes which break up authority and respect;
threats to our position which make us oppressors;
oppressive regimes which make us timid.

Help us too to fight with the right weapons:

Fasten on the belt of truth; for coat of mail put on integrity.
Lord, help us to speak the truth to each other in Christian fellowship,
and make us truthful, honest and consistent in our daily life.

Let the shoes on your feet be the gospel of peace.
Lord, help us to play our part in your great work of reconciliation. As
Jewish and Gentile Christians once found their peace in Christ, so
may Christians help to heal the divisions of our world.

Take up the great shield of faith.
Lord, help us to keep you steadily in view in every crisis. Whatever
changes, you do not change.

Take salvation for helmet.
Lord, make us ready to take risks for your sake, knowing that both we
and our loved ones are safe in your hands.

*For sword, take that which the Spirit gives you – the words that come
from God.*
Lord, give us words to say: words that will encourage, words that will
comfort, words that will persuade.

Pray on every occasion in the power of the Spirit.
Lord, we pray for those whom we cannot help otherwise, because you
love them, and you can lead them in the way they should go.

The whole armour of God – II

Lord God, we give thanks together for the double wonder of your presence among men and your mercy towards men.

You are Lord of eternity, yet you make your dwelling with the sons of time.

You are the holy Lord, yet you seek out the company of sinners.

Here today, in our humble recollection and looking forward, we acknowledge that everything comes from your generosity. It is your love which has kindled love – love in each of us for one another, love in all of us for the foretaste of heaven which we have in the fellowship of your church and in the service of the world.

And we pray that you will help us take up those gifts and graces which your love provides, so that we may not be overcome by the onslaughts of evil.

Help us to fasten on the belt of truth, and for coat of mail to put on integrity. It is so easy for little pretences to mount up so that we become altogether a sham, and for us to be trapped by temptations we intended only to flirt with. Give us firm footing in the gospel of peace, so that we do not lose contact with reality or forget that high principles are no use without action.

And because we are vulnerable in heart and head, be yourself our shield and helmet, and give us words to wield in your cause – strong promises of Christ, prayers in which to shape before you our hopes and our resolves.

We bring before you in prayer now our friends near and far, our families, our church. In your mercy may our love reach out to those who are not here, in whatever joy or sorrow they find themselves today.

We pray for those who must face violence or family upheaval; for those maimed or bereaved by sudden disaster; for those also whose struggle is not against outward circumstances but against inward demons of disappointment, envy, frustrated ambition, lack of security and love.

Hear our prayers. Make us people alert to hear and heed unspoken calls

for help. And let our fellowship with those who have gone before us
in the faith give us a sense of proportion, lest we be daunted and overwhelmed. Bring us back to the centre of our confidence as we name
the name of him through whom these and all our prayers are made –
Jesus Christ our Saviour.

234

The massacre of the innocents

Father of peace and God of love, we cannot well believe that the coming
of your blessed Son was the effective cause of the deaths of innocent
children. Yet we see it to be still true of our world that great changes
meet violent resistance. There are tears as well as smiles in Christmas;
for the road to Bethlehem is also the road to Calvary. There is
innocent death after all, and we cannot but weep.

Yet we hear the Lord saying, 'Do not weep for me: weep for your-
selves'; and once again we come to understand that his victory must
mean the overthrow of our own sovereignty over our lives.

Father, make of us and of all men what you would have us be. Bring us
through the night of tears to the morning of joy. Help us to be ready
for great upheaval in the course of establishing your kingdom. Let
the discords in the Christmas story warn us that the snowfall of the
gospel is no gentle blanket, leaving the familiar outlines softened
and sanctified, but more like a blizzard, driving against and past
the defences we have put up, swirling in our eyes until it fills our
vision and forces us to leave our false security and seek our true
destiny.

Lord, when you master our self-will we shall become ourselves. When
you take us in hand we shall discover life's purpose. Turn us round,
and give us new direction and a safe path into the future, for the
sake of Jesus Christ our Lord.

Happiness

Happiness is the stream whose rapids are elation and whose still pools
are contentment.

Its spring is among the green uplands of innocence, but it flows
longest along the valley of self-forgetfulness.

From those who are looking for it, it is often hidden: but they whose
thought is for others are continually surprised by gleams and glimpses
of it.

Travellers upon its waters may expect to be carried at times through
dark caverns and fearsome gorges: yet they find that each obstacle
that would hold it back serves only to deepen its channel and
strengthen its course.

From God it comes and to God it goes: and across the harbour mouth,
where it enters the sea, is written in shining letters, 'Enter into the
joy of your Lord.'

Make us, Lord,
      happy in doing your will,
      unhappy in flouting it;
      happy when right and truth prevail,
      unhappy when others suffer pain or injustice.
May we guard as precious gifts both laughter and tears
    and be human towards one another
    as you, Lord, were human towards us,
    and are, and always will be.

X

Times and Seasons

236

Christmas

We thank you, Father, that once again it is Christmas.
We thank you for presents and cards, for Christmas dinner and parties,
    for visits to other people and other people to stay with us.
It's a great time of the year, and we are very glad.
And we thank you that for once we are not thinking of how important
    or clever or kind we are, but of how much we owe to you for giving
    us Jesus.
How wise he was! How brave he was! How important he has become!
He has taken us all on, to make us what you want us to be.
Although we have heard this so many times before, it is still staggering.
Make us more and more glad and more and more thankful as the years
    go by.

237

Christmas

Heavenly Father, as we sing our Christmas-time praise our own words
    condemn us.
We are thanking you for sending Jesus to show us how life ought to be
    lived: but we have not often really tried to live like him.
    Forgive us, Father.

We are thanking you for making it clear to us in Jesus that there is no
limit to your love for us: but we are always setting limits on our love
for you and for one another.
Forgive us, Father.

We are thanking you for keeping your promises, made to Abraham and
the people of long ago: but there are many times when we do not keep
our promises. Sometimes we cannot, because we have promised too
much. Sometimes we could, but do not because it is too much
trouble.
Forgive us, Father.

Have mercy on our whole human race, which so often seems to carry
on as if Jesus had never lived among us. And write upon our hearts
the truth of this saying, that Christ Jesus came into the world to
save sinners. We ask it for his sake.

238

Christmas

God our Father, we thank you for the joy and wonder of this day;
for the long ages of preparation as your world unfolded its variety
and you gave birth to mankind; and then the further preparing of
man, through the experience of your covenant-mercies, until the
time had come for you to send your Son and so reveal your face.
May the church of Jesus have the character of Jesus. May our words of
homage today be borne out by our actions every day.
We pray for families united today; and for families sundered by illness
or injury or estrangement.
We pray, Father, that in this world of yours and ours, justice may be
done to the human rights of all, and that upon that foundation you
will build true peace for us. Help each one of us to be a doer of
justice and a maker of peace. May we love mercy and ever walk
humbly with you and with one another: so that at the last your plan
may be fulfilled indeed, and all men worship you in the brotherhood
of eternity in the one Name of our salvation, Jesus Christ the Lord.

The end of the year

The wells of his compassion never run dry. His mercies have been
renewed for us every morning of our lives.
Father, help us to love one another as you have loved us, without keeping any score of wrongs.
In penitence and hope we bring before you this year that is coming to
an end. We remember with what clear resolve we began it; and we
confess the sorry sight it soon became, dulled over with deceits and
evasions and doing down others so as to lever ourselves up.
Father, forgive us the sins we knew as we committed them, and forgive
us the sins we did not know, which still did harm.
If we are fit for it, use us in the setting right of what we have helped to
make wrong. So crown this year with your goodness: then we shall
know it to have been indeed a year of grace – a year of our Lord,
Jesus Christ.

240

An intercession at Epiphany or a Baptism

Father, as we remember how our Lord Jesus was identified by Baptism
with John's movement of repentance and renewal, we pray for the
renewal of humanity today, and for the church as a means of renewal.
We pray for the welfare of nations and the wisdom of governments, for
social justice and for racial harmony. May laws and policies dignify
man, not degrade him: and may the arrival of your kingdom in
Jesus be attested by the witness of Christians in every walk of life.
We pray for all who suffer loss, and who are diminished by illness, by
disappointment, or by the attitude of their fellow men. Support and
strengthen these and all who are in the wilderness facing the testing
of what they believe in.
And we pray for all who must die soon – both those who know it and
those who do not. Confirm in every one of us that it is not for this life
only that we have hope in Christ: and in the communion of holy

things may we find bonds forged between us that endure to all
eternity.
Through Jesus Christ our Lord.

241

A prayer at Passiontide, Easter or Eucharist

Lord Jesus Christ, your light shines on in the dark, and the darkness
has never mastered it. You are the King of glory, yet your glory is
not to be served but to serve. You are the King of love, and your
love is to give yourself a ransom for many. You suffer what looks
like defeat, and emerge victorious. Your power comes to its full
strength in weakness.

Into the light of this kingship of yours we bring, in prayer, the hopes
and needs of your brother men.

We pray for those whose task it is to make peace where there is conflict,
and to give leadership where many voices urge different points of
view. Help them to be true to what they themselves believe, yet to be
ready also to be led deeper into your revelation about man, and to
modify their ideas by what you bring them to perceive.

We pray for all who fall victim to the violence and passion with which
others pursue their principles, or who from any other cause endure
today the agony of bereavement, or of physical suffering, or of
anxiety for the safety of their dear ones. Lord, we believe that you
have made a path even through this darkness. Be close beside those
who find themselves there now.

We pray for your church, that everywhere its fellowship and its actions
may more and more embody your vision, and extend your gospel into
our present times. May all who acknowledge themselves your people
be transformed by the renewing of their minds, so that they may
think for you, speak for you, and work for you, perceiving your
Father's will and ever tending towards its height.

And to you, Lord Jesus Christ, with God the Father and the Holy
Spirit, be praise and adoration from the church on earth and from
the church in heaven, for ever and ever.

An intercession on Palm Sunday

The versicle and response, 'Lord, in your mercy/Hear our prayer', may be used after each paragraph of this prayer.

God our Father, your moment comes still, to men and to nations, when your Holy Spirit brings home to them the nature of true kingship and the methods of heavenly power. May your church everywhere have such a vision of Jesus – so focus upon him and so proclaim him – that your moment may be recognized whenever it comes, and your Son be greeted as King and all the triumphs of love extended.

We pray for the nations and their leaders – Europe; Russia and China; America; the Commonwealth; the Third World. Especially we pray that those whose quest for power is pursued by means of war or terrorism may come to accept from Christ, the Prince of Peace, a new scale of human values.

We pray for all who suffer – the victims of accident, malice or mindlessness; those bearing the burden of painful illness, whether physical or mental; those caught in intolerable webs of fear and perplexity; those whom guilt or loyalty has shut up in the dark. May Christ the High Priest, who passed this way himself, be known to them as a living Saviour bringing healing and liberation.

Finally, we pray for the coming of the kingdom of heaven on earth in all its completeness, when Hosanna shall never give way to Crucify, when all that hurts and destroys shall be finished and forgotten, and all tears shall be wiped away save tears of joy. Father, keep us within the great fellowship of expectation and hope on earth and of peace and fulfilment in heaven.

243

Prayer on a summer Sunday

God our Father, we come to worship you today in thankfulness for the
beauty of the earth and sky. The heavens declare your glory and the
green trees speak your power and grace.

We thank you for all the good gifts of yours that lift up our hearts and
make us glad to be alive: and we pray for our friends who are away
on holiday this weekend, that they may find joy and contentment,
rest and renewal.

We pray also for those to whom the morning sunlight means only
another day of fear, or pain, or worry, or loneliness. Father, reveal to
their hearts that Jesus Christ is the Lord, able to take away the sins
of the world and to assuage its griefs. May his glorious presence
dawn on all darkness and comfort every sorrow.

And may we who worship you now in his name become day by day
more hospitable to his spirit, so that the church everywhere may live
as his body and show the results of his kingship.

244

Before a church council

Lord God, our heavenly Father, we thank you that in Jesus of Nazareth
the world has at last a king who rules in righteousness, a man who is
refuge from the wind and shelter from the tempest.

May we, and all who profess the name of Christian, be enabled by
your Spirit to be in the world as he was; so that your church, too,
may be like the shadow of a great rock in a thirsty land.

We gather now in our Lord's name to take counsel together concerning
his work. Give us seeing eyes and listening ears, understanding minds
and willing hearts.

May we be so inwardly renewed by our faith that we are able to form
noble designs and stand firm in that nobility, and so play the part
you have for us in the fulfilling of your purpose.

Through Jesus Christ our Lord.

(Based on Isaiah 32.1–8 NEB)

245

Before a church counci.

Almighty Father, giver of wisdom, peace and power: grant that in this
(council of your church) our thinking may partake of your wisdom,
our speaking may exemplify your peace, and our deciding may serve
the purposes of your power at work among us.
Through Jesus Christ our Lord.

246

Before a church council

Here we are, our Father, the different people that you made us. We
come to worship you with varieties of gifts but the same Spirit.
Our meeting together today is part of our obedience to our Lord Jesus
Christ, and to the call he has given to each one of us to follow him.
Help us therefore to be subject to one another out of reverence for
Christ. Let each look not only to his or her own interests, but to the
interests of all and to the hope of your coming kingdom in our
community.
We pray for our absent friends – for their peace and safety. And for all
who must grieve or suffer at the present time we pray, that they may
find comfort in the presence and compassion of people who have your
grace in their hearts.
Bless now our hearing and our speaking, so that the fellowship of our
hearts and minds may serve the purposes of your love.
Through Jesus Christ our Lord.

Index of Subjects